1,√0

D1718494

STARK

Original-Prüfungsaufgaben

2017

TRAINING QUALI

Lösungen

Englisch

Bayern

2011–2016

STARK

© 2016 Stark Verlag GmbH
11. neu bearbeitete und ergänzte Auflage
www.stark-verlag.de

Inhalt

Autorin: Birgit Mohr

Vorwort

Liebe Schülerin, lieber Schüler,

dieses Buch ist das Lösungsheft zu dem Band **Training Quali Englisch Bayern** (Bestellnummer 93555).
Die Lösungen bzw. Lösungsvorschläge in diesem Buch ermöglichen es dir, deine Leistung einzuschätzen. Durch die **Hinweise** zu einzelnen Aufgaben lernst du, was bei einer bestimmten Aufgabenstellung von dir erwartet wird.

Viel Erfolg im Quali wünscht dir

Birgit Mohr

✔ **Allgemeiner Hinweis:** *Zum Lösen aller folgenden Aufgaben zum Kapitel „Listening" musst du dir den Text jeweils genau anhören. Wenn du ihn nach dem ersten Hören noch nicht verstanden hast, kannst du ihn dir natürlich auch öfter anhören. Lies dir den Hörverstehenstext nur durch, wenn du mit den Lösungen ganz unsicher bist und gar nicht weiterkommst.*

Listening Comprehension Test 1: In the supermarket

1 Dear customers, welcome to Richie's Supermarket, where you can always get a bargain!
This week we are celebrating health week at Richie's Supermarket, and we take special care to offer you the best products for the health of your whole family at
5 the best prices you can find!
In our fruit and vegetable department, you can pick your choice of the best apples, pears or tomatoes for just 59 pence per kilo! Yes, that's one kilo of apples, pears or tomatoes for just 59 pence! By the way, the 5 kilogram bag of potatoes now costs only 1 pound 79.
10 Or, if you are looking for some relaxing moments, why don't you visit our cosmetics department, where you will find a wide selection of natural bath products for just 99 pence each. Imagine, you can take a refreshing, relaxing bath, with the fragrance of your choice, for just 99 pence! What's more, all sun lotions are now reduced by 25 %.
15 Dear customers, at Richie's Supermarket we care for your health. Take your time to find out about our offers, and enjoy your health week with us!

Aufgabe 1

a) Richie's
   ✔ Hinweis: Z. 1
b) health week
   ✔ Hinweis: Z. 3

Aufgabe 2

a) 59 pence
   ✔ Hinweis: Z. 6 f.

1

b) 1 pound 79 pence
   ✒ **Hinweis:** *Z. 8 f.*

c) 99 pence
   ✒ **Hinweis:** *Z. 11 f.*

d) 25 %
   ✒ **Hinweis:** *Z. 13 f.*

Aufgabe 3

a) *wrong:* protests, *correct:* products

b) *wrong:* friend, *correct:* fruit

c) *wrong:* normal, *correct:* natural

d) *wrong:* money, *correct:* time

Listening Comprehension Test 2: At the airport

1 **Part 1: At the check-in**

MR MILLER: Good afternoon, my wife and I have tickets to Munich. I hope we are not too late for the flight.

WOMAN AT SERVICE DESK: Please give me your tickets and your passports.

5 MR MILLER: Here they are.

WOMAN AT SERVICE DESK: Thank you. OK, let me check …

WOMAN AT SERVICE DESK: Mr and Mrs Miller – you are going to Munich via Frankfurt?

MR MILLER: Yes, we have to change planes in Frankfurt.

10 WOMAN AT SERVICE DESK: OK, you are still on time for the flight to Frankfurt. But you have to hurry – the plane is going to take off in 20 minutes! Where would you like to sit in the plane, by the window or on the aisle?

MR MILLER: On the aisle, please.

WOMAN AT SERVICE DESK: No problem. I am giving you two seats in the centre
15 row – one of them is next to the aisle. Would you like to check in any luggage?

MR MILLER: No, thanks, we have only hand luggage.

WOMAN AT SERVICE DESK: OK.

WOMAN AT SERVICE DESK: Here are your boarding cards to Frankfurt, and from Frankfurt to Munich. Please proceed to Gate 17 immediately.

20 MR MILLER: Thank you.

WOMAN AT SERVICE DESK: Enjoy your flight!

Aufgabe 1

a) true
   / **Hinweis:** *Z. 2*

b) false
   / **Hinweis:** *Z. 4 f.*

c) false
   / **Hinweis:** *Z. 13*

d) false
   / **Hinweis:** *Z. 16*

Aufgabe 2

a) their tickets and passports
   / **Hinweis:** *Z. 4*

b) in Frankfurt
   / **Hinweis:** *Z. 9*

c) in 20 minutes
   / **Hinweis:** *Z. 11*

d) 17
   / **Hinweis:** *Z. 19*

1 **Part 2: Boarding the plane**
   (Busy sounds of passengers boarding the plane)
   WOMAN: Excuse me, sir?
   MR MILLER: Who? Me?
5 WOMAN: Yes, sir. Excuse me, I'm sorry to bother you but it looks like you are sitting in my seat.
   MR MILLER: Oh, really? Let me check our boarding cards ...
   (Rustling in his travel bag.)
   MR MILLER: Hmm, where are they ... just a moment.
10 WOMAN: Sure, no hurry.
   MR MILLER: Ah, here they are. Let me just check ... Here, please take a look, my wife and I have seats 21D and 21E. Which seat do you have?
   WOMAN: Oops, that's strange. My seat number is 21E, too!
   MR MILLER: This is very strange. It must be the airline's mistake!
15 WOMAN *(sighing)*: It must be! Wait a moment, I'm just going to ask the flight attendant.
   (Some time passes.)

FLIGHT ATTENDANT: Hello, sir! This lady tells me that you have the same seat as
she does. Could you please show me your boarding cards?
20 MR MILLER: Yes, of course. Here, these are the boarding cards for my wife and
myself.
FLIGHT ATTENDANT: 21D and 21E ... Mr and Mrs Miller ... The flight number and
date are correct. You really are sitting in the right seat. Could you show me
your boarding card again, please?
25 WOMAN: OK, here it is.
FLIGHT ATTENDANT: Ah, that's it! This boarding card is for another flight. Look, it
has the same flight number, but the date was two weeks ago! Did you travel to
Frankfurt two weeks ago, too?
WOMAN: Oh, yes, you're right, excuse me. This is my fault, it's the wrong board-
30 ing card. I travel to Frankfurt every two weeks and that's an old one. Let me
just check in my bag ...
FLIGHT ATTENDANT: No problem for you, Mr and Mrs Miller, you have the right
seats.
MR MILLER: OK, thank you.
35 WOMAN: I'm afraid I can't find my boarding card, I don't know where I put it.
FLIGHT ATTENDANT: That's no problem. Please come with me and I will look up
your seat on the computer. *(Voice fading)* It's not the first time that somebody
lost their boarding card on the way from the gate to the plane ...

Aufgabe 3

a) B
  ∕ **Hinweis:** *Z. 5f.*

b) A
  ∕ **Hinweis:** *Z. 14*

c) C
  ∕ **Hinweis:** *Z. 22f.*

d) C
  ∕ **Hinweis:** *Z. 26*

e) B
  ∕ **Hinweis:** *Z. 35*

Aufgabe 4

a) 21E

b) (the) boarding card(s)

4

c) 2/two weeks before/ago

d) (on the) computer

Listening Comprehension Test 3: Mrs Brown at the shoe store

1 **Part 1**

SHOP ASSISTANT: Hello, how can I help you?

MRS BROWN: Hello, I'm looking for a pair of shoes for the summer.

SHOP ASSISTANT: Do you have something specific in mind?

5 MRS BROWN *(hesitantly)*: Mm, yes. I'd like a pair of comfortable leather shoes.

SHOP ASSISTANT: What colour are you looking for?

MRS BROWN: A light colour please, maybe white or beige.

SHOP ASSISTANT: OK, please come over to our summer section.

Aufgabe 1

a) summer
   / Hinweis: Z. 3

b) comfortable
   / Hinweis: Z. 5

c) beige
   / Hinweis: Z. 7

1 **Part 2**

SHOP ASSISTANT: Here, take a look at this pair. They are a new design from Italy and are very comfortable. Are these the type of shoes you like to wear?

MRS BROWN: Not exactly. These shoes are too high – I don't think I could wear

5   them for more than an hour. I also don't like it that my toes show. I'd like a closed pair of shoes that I can wear with socks.

SHOP ASSISTANT: Of course. Please come over to this aisle, where we have the more casual shoes.

SHOP ASSISTANT *(after a moment)*: Here, please have a look. What do you think of

10   these loafers, which are a nice beige? These are from another collection from Italy.

MRS BROWN: Oh, yes, they do look nice! I think I'd like to try them.

SHOP ASSISTANT: What size can I get for you?

MRS BROWN: That would be a 5, thank you.

5

Aufgabe 2

a) toes

   ✏ **Hinweis:** Z. 5

b) socks

   ✏ **Hinweis:** Z. 6

c) Italy

   ✏ **Hinweis:** Z. 10 ff.

Part 3

1 SHOP ASSISTANT: How do the shoes fit? Do they feel comfortable?

MRS BROWN: Phew, I'm afraid they don't fit. Have you got them half a size larger?

SHOP ASSISTANT: One moment, I'll go to the back again to look. I'm not sure that

5 we still have this style in 5 ½, I think we've already sold all of them. *(pause while he goes to look)*

MRS BROWN: And, have you got them in 5 ½?

SHOP ASSISTANT: Sorry, I'm afraid not. Size 5 ½ is completely sold out. But I did bring you a size 6. Would you like to have a try?

10 MRS BROWN: Oh, that's a pity ... but OK, I'll try them.

MRS BROWN *(after a moment)*: Let's see ...

SHOP ASSISTANT: What do you think, do they fit nicely?

MRS BROWN: Yes, I think they do fit! But I'm a bit surprised that I'm a size 6 now!

SHOP ASSISTANT: Don't worry, this make is sometimes a bit tighter than others.

15 MRS BROWN: OK ... Well, I've made up my mind – I would like to buy these shoes.

SHOP ASSISTANT: Perfect!

Aufgabe 3

a) fit

   ✏ **Hinweis:** Z. 3

b) 5.5/5 ½

   ✏ **Hinweis:** Z. 3 ff.

c) 6

   ✏ **Hinweis:** Z. 13 ff.

6

Part 4

GIRL AT CASH REGISTER: Hello, how are you today? What would you like to pay for?

MRS BROWN: That pair of beige loafers, please.

5 GIRL AT CASH REGISTER: OK.

GIRL AT CASH REGISTER: That'll be forty-nine ninety-five. Would you like to pay by cash or credit card?

MRS BROWN: I'd like to pay by credit card, please. Here you are.

GIRL AT CASH REGISTER: Thanks!

10 GIRL AT CASH REGISTER: So, here are your shoes. Thanks very much. Goodbye now.

MRS BROWN: Thanks. Goodbye!

Aufgabe 4

a) true
   / Hinweis: Z. 4

b) false
   / Hinweis: Z. 6

c) true
   / Hinweis: Z. 8

Listening Comprehension Test 4: Visit to Stirling Castle

1 **Part 1**

(Conversation starts between two teenagers on back seat of a car)

TABBY: Nick, you've been playing that game for hours now, could you please turn it off?

5 NICK *(sounding absent)*: No.

TABBY: Nick, please! I don't want to hear that sound anymore. Could you turn it off, now!?

NICK *(concentrating on his game)*: Sorry, Tabby, I can't turn it off, now ... I have to finish this level first.

10 TABBY: Please!

NICK *(after a moment)*: There you go, I finally made it to level fourteen! Wow! *(pause)*

NICK: What a bummer, it looks like the rain out there is never going to end. Anyway, do you know where Mum and Dad are driving us to?

15 TABBY: Sure, I've been reading all about it in this travel guide, while you were playing that stupid game. We're driving to Stirling Castle – ever heard of it?

NICK: Yes, I think we learned about Stirling Castle in history class. Isn't it the most important castle in Scotland?

TABBY: Yes, it is. It's one of the largest and most important castles of the country.
20 Several Scottish kings and queens were crowned at Stirling Castle, for example Mary, Queen of Scots, in 1543. She also lived there with her family.

NICK: Was that the same queen as Mary Stuart?

TABBY: Yes, Mary, Queen of Scots, and Mary Stuart were the same person. Didn't you know that? Anyway, did you know that when Mary, Queen of Scots, was
25 crowned she was still a baby?

NICK: No, really?

TABBY: Yes. That was because her father, King James V, died shortly after she was born.

NICK: Hmmm ... interesting. What else does your travel guide tell us about Stir-
30 ling Castle?

TABBY: Here ... Did you know that many people claim to have seen ghosts at Stirling Castle?

NICK: Really? That sounds cool.

TABBY: Yes. Listen to this: Several ghosts have reportedly been seen at Stirling
35 Castle. The one seen most often is the so-called Highland Ghost. He was seen by both staff and visitors, and he was wearing a traditional Scottish costume. Some tourists first thought he was a tour guide, but then they saw him turn around, walk away and vanish in front of their eyes!

NICK: Wow!

40 TABBY: And listen to this (reading excitedly): The Green Lady is another famous ghost in Stirling Castle. The legend is that she was a servant girl to Mary, Queen of Scots. One night while the queen was sleeping, and the servant girl was with her, the curtains of the queen's bed caught fire from a candle. Although she was able to save the queen's life, the servant girl was badly injured
45 and died. Ever since, from time to time, a ghost has been seen in the castle, wearing green clothes – the same colour as the servant girl's clothes. This is why the ghost is called the Green Lady. And there are still some more ghosts ...

NICK: Aha. Well, Tabby, let's see if we can find some of them at the castle ...

50 TABBY (giving Nick a punch): Stop it, Nick, you're so dumb. I'm frightened by all of these stories already!

Aufgabe 1

a) Scotland
   Hinweis: Z. 17 f.

b) the same person.
   Hinweis: Z. 23

c) was still a baby.
   Hinweis: Z. 24 f.

d) "Highland Ghost".
   Hinweis: Z. 35 f.

e) was badly injured when saving the queen's life.
   Hinweis: Z. 42 ff.

f) clothes.
   Hinweis: Z. 45 f.

1 **Part 2**

TOUR GUIDE: And now I would like to welcome you to the palace of Stirling Castle. It is one of the most remarkable Renaissance buildings in Britain. The palace was built in 1540 for King James V. The Scottish kings and queens used
5 this palace as a royal residence until 1603. In 1603, King James VI also became King of England, and the royal court moved to London.

A few years ago, the palace of Stirling Castle was completely renovated for 12 million pounds. Artists from many countries made the interior look like it could have been in the 16th century, when Mary, Queen of Scots, was running
10 around in the palace as a young girl. So the paintings and pieces of furniture you see in this hall are not the originals from the 16th century. This is why they have such a beautiful, fresh colour. *(fading)*

NICK *(whispers)*: Wow, Tabby, this is the greatest castle I've ever seen!

TABBY *(whispers back)*: Haven't I told you?

15 NICK: Yeah ...

TOUR GUIDE *(fading in)*: In the castle you can also meet costumed characters, who demonstrate to the visitors what life in the palace and at the royal court was like in the 16th century. As you walk through the rooms, you will see servants, musicians, ambassadors and all sorts of characters.

20 NICK *(whispers)*: Cool, let's have a look and find some of these costumed characters.

TABBY *(whispers back)*: Yes, let's try!

Aufgabe 2

a) in 1540
  / **Hinweis:** *Z. 3 f.*

b) in 1603
  / **Hinweis:** *Z. 4 ff.*

c) to London
  / **Hinweis:** *Z. 5 f.*

d) 12 million pounds
  / **Hinweis:** *Z. 7 f.*

e) (They have a beautiful and) fresh colour.
  / **Hinweis:** *Z. 11 f.*

f) (the) 16th century
  / **Hinweis:** *Z. 16 ff.*

₁ Part 3

NICK: Here, Tabby, let's stand under this archway. It's really too bad we left the umbrella inside the car!

TABBY: I wonder where Mum and Dad are now. I hope they aren't looking for
₅ us ... Gosh, I'm all wet and cold!

NICK: I think they're still inside the palace, or in the souvenir shop. It's a pretty long tour, don't you think?

TABBY: Good for them, so they're at least inside! I told you we shouldn't have left the tour.

₁₀ NICK: Let's go inside here for a moment. It's drier in there.

TABBY: Yes, it is.

NICK: Tabby, look!

TABBY: What?

NICK: There is another one of those costumed characters from the palace, over
₁₅ there in the shadow ... She looks like a servant.

TABBY: What? Where? I can't see anyone.

NICK: Right there! Don't you see her? She's carrying something ...

TABBY: *Where?* I don't see her!

NICK *(screams)*: Ahh!

₂₀ TABBY: Nick, what happened? Did you step on something?

NICK: T ... T ... Tabby, you won't believe what I just saw!

TABBY *(frightened)*: What? What did you see?

10

NICK: T ... T ... The servant girl! Sh ... Sh ... She was standing there just a moment ago. She was carrying a basket or something. But then she just turned around and walked right into that wall.

TABBY *(screams)*: Ahh! What? Are you serious?

NICK: Yes! I ... I ... saw her ... She was wearing a green dress and a white apron ...

TABBY: Oh my God! Let's get out of here!

NICK: Right, let's leave this place!

TABBY: Oh my God! This is scary!!!

Aufgabe 3

0	1	2	3	4
A	C	D	G	I

Part 4

(In the car)

TABBY: You are such an idiot! I'll never tell you anything about any place we visit, ever again.

NICK: *(laughing)*

TABBY: You idiot!

NICK *(laughing)*: Sorry, it was just so funny ... you should have seen your face. The moment I told you the costumed servant disappeared into the wall ...

TABBY: Stop it! I hate you!

NICK: *(laughing)*

TABBY: For a moment I really believed you and thought there was a ghost!

NICK: *(laughing)* That was funny, wasn't it?

TABBY: Don't ever, ever do that again!

NICK: OK, I won't.

TABBY: Promise?

NICK: Sure, I promise. *(cracks up again and continues to laugh)*

TABBY: Ahh! I don't believe you! I swear I will NEVER go into ANY castle with you again!

Aufgabe 4

a) *wrong:* idiom, *correct:* idiot

b) *wrong:* teach, *correct:* tell

c) *wrong:* not, *correct:* just

d) *wrong:* trusted, *correct:* believed

e) *wrong:* palace, *correct:* castle

Aufgabe 1

Beispiellösungen:

a) At school you find chalk, <u>a blackboard</u> and <u>pupils</u>, for example.

b) When it is cold in winter there is <u>snow</u> and <u>ice</u>.

c) In the zoo there are a lot of animals, for example <u>monkeys</u>, <u>tigers</u> and <u>bears</u>.

Aufgabe 2

Beispiellösungen:

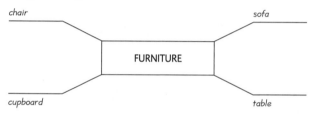

Aufgabe 3

✏ **Hinweis:** *In dieser Aufgabe ist der Oberbegriff nicht vorgegeben. Du musst über-legen, was die aufgelisteten Wörter bzw. die Bilder gemeinsam haben.*

a) colours

b) musical instruments

c) languages

Aufgabe 4

✎ **Hinweis:** *Zu Beginn jeder Zeile ist der Oberbegriff vorgegeben. Du musst also nur noch überlegen, welches Wort nicht dazu passt.*

a) pineapple
  ✎ **Hinweis:** *kein Gemüse*

b) horse
  ✎ **Hinweis:** *kein Fahrzeug*

c) vinegar
  ✎ **Hinweis:** *kein Getränk*

d) fork
  ✎ **Hinweis:** *keine Mahlzeit*

e) soft
  ✎ **Hinweis:** *keine Geschmacksrichtung*

Aufgabe 5

✎ **Hinweis:** *Hier musst du überlegen, welches Wort nicht in die Reihe passt, und was die verbliebenen Wörter gemeinsam haben.*

a) b̶a̶g̶ → clothes
  ✎ **Hinweis:** *„bag" ist kein Kleidungsstück*

b) p̶e̶n̶ → car/bus/van/vehicles
  ✎ **Hinweis:** *„pen" ist kein Teil eines Fahrzeugs*

c) f̶o̶o̶d̶ → parts of the body
  ✎ **Hinweis:** *„food" ist kein Körperteil*

d) k̶n̶i̶f̶e̶ → vegetables
  ✎ **Hinweis:** *„knife" ist kein Gemüse*

e) m̶e̶a̶t̶ → desserts
  ✎ **Hinweis:** *„meat" ist kein Nachtisch*

Aufgabe 6

a) restaurant
b) theatre
c) hospital
d) church
e) park

Aufgabe 7

board	–	bored
whole	–	hole
no	–	know
break	–	brake
hour	–	our
piece	–	peace
see	–	sea

Aufgabe 8

a) It was dark at • in • over the morning when I went to school.

b) The plane was left • late • soon this morning.

c) I often drive • go • miss by train.

d) What • Which • Where can I buy a watch, please?

Aufgabe 9

a) ugly

b) wet

c) sell

d) low

e) wide

f) sunny/dry

g) start/begin

h) clean

i) hot

j) day

k) down

l) fast/quick

m) asleep

n) sad/unhappy

Hinweis: *Im Englischen haben nur wenige Nomen eine eigene „weibliche" Form. Oft wird das Nomen (z. B. „teacher" = „Lehrer"/„Lehrerin") durch ein Pronomen (z. B. „he"/„his" oder „she"/„her") oder eine Ergänzung (z. B. „Mrs/Ms", „Mr") näher bestimmt, sodass klar ist, ob es sich um eine weibliche oder männliche Person handelt.*

a) policewoman

b) princess

c) actress

d) waitress

Aufgabe 11

a) knives

b) mice

c) men

d) women

e) children

f) fish

g) leaves

h) teeth

Aufgabe 12

a) railway station

b) travel agency

c) suitcase

d) passport

Aufgabe 13

a) a radio

b) a pen

c) a mobile phone

d) a key

Aufgabe 14

a) Big Ben is a tourist **attraction** in London.

b) The "Anne Frank House" is in Amsterdam. That is in the Netherlands. The people there are called the **D**utch.

c) The Leaning Tower of Pisa is in Italy. The people there **speak** Italian.

d) The Eiffel Tower is in Paris. Paris is the **c**apital of France.

e) The Puerta del Sol is in Madrid, in Spain. People from Spain are called **S**panish.

Aufgabe 15

✦ **Hinweis:** *Die Antworten geben dir Aufschluss darüber, welches Fragewort du verwenden musst.*

a) Where is the cafeteria?

b) How much is a sandwich?

c) Who is that girl over there?

d) Why is she looking so sad?

e) When did she move?

Aufgabe 16

✦ **Hinweis:** *Zur Kontrolle, ob du die Lücken korrekt ausgefüllt hast, lies dir am Ende den gesamten Text noch einmal durch. Wenn du merkst, dass manche Sätze keinen Sinn ergeben, musst du dir andere Lösungsmöglichkeiten überlegen.*

a) CLARA: Hi Eric, how are you?

b) ERIC: Fine, thanks. How are you?

c) CLARA: I'm fine, too. But I miss you all.

d) ERIC: We miss you, too. When are you coming home?

e) CLARA: On Friday.

f) ERIC: We're looking forward to seeing you.

Aufgabe 17

✦ **Hinweis:** *Hier musst du nicht auf die Verwendung der richtigen Zeit achten, da alle Verben in der Grundform (Infinitiv) eingesetzt werden.*

"I'm going to <u>wear</u> my suit and I <u>think</u> I will be very nervous. I <u>hope</u> I won't <u>forget</u> my lines. Even my grandparents <u>want</u> to come and <u>see</u> me acting. I hope everyone will <u>enjoy</u> the evening."

Aufgabe 18

SARA: "Lisa and I are going <u>to</u> Paris on 12th May."
PIERRE: "When <u>will</u> you arrive in Paris?"
SARA: "At 2.35 pm."
PIERRE: "<u>What</u> is the name of the hotel you're staying at?"
SARA: "<u>It's</u> Hôtel de Paris."
PIERRE: "Do you have any <u>plans</u> for your stay?"
SARA: "I want to do some <u>shopping/sightseeing</u> and visit the Eiffel Tower and the Champs-Elysées."
PIERRE: "I would like <u>to show you</u> the nightlife in Paris. I'm looking <u>forward</u> to seeing you next <u>week</u>."

Aufgabe 19

✏ **Hinweis:** *Für die Verwendung der Präpositionen gibt es keine festen Regeln. Am besten lernst du die jeweiligen Präpositionen immer zusammen mit den entsprechenden Verben. In der Grammatik findest du ab Seite 81 eine Übersicht über häufige Präpositionen im Englischen.*

a) The teacher is sitting <u>at</u> the table.

b) John has never been <u>to</u> the United States.

c) What do you think <u>of</u>/<u>about</u> bungee jumping?

d) The new girl in our class is <u>from</u> Brighton.

e) I am waiting <u>for</u> you at the station.

Aufgabe 20

✏ **Hinweis:** *Das Present progressive findest du auf Seite 87 in der Grammatik.*

a) What are you <u>doing</u> in this picture?

b) I <u>am carrying</u> a large watermelon I bought at the market.

c) The dress I <u>am wearing</u> in this picture is new.

d) The sun <u>is shining</u> in every picture.

e) Here we <u>are going</u> down to the beach.

Aufgabe 21

✏ **Hinweis:** *Die Regeln zur Verwendung des Going-to-future kannst du in der Grammatik auf Seite 90 nachlesen.*

a) <u>I am going to meet</u> Jane on Saturday for breakfast.

b) On Monday I <u>am going to see</u> the doctor.

c) I <u>am going to go</u> camping with some of my friends.

Aufgabe 22

✏ **Hinweis:** *Das Simple past findest du auf Seite 88 der Grammatik.*

On Saturday morning Kelly and Sara <u>met</u> in town to do some shopping. They <u>were</u> invited to a birthday party in the evening and <u>wanted</u> to buy a present. At first they <u>couldn't</u> really decide what to buy, but then they <u>saw</u> a cool smartphone case and <u>were</u> sure that that would be the right present for Tim. Now they <u>could</u> take a look around for some trendy clothes for the party. Kelly <u>bought</u> a T-shirt, but Sara <u>didn't</u> find anything. Afterwards they <u>went</u> home to get changed for the party.

Aufgabe 23

✏ **Hinweis:** *Hier musst du entscheiden, welche Zeitform korrekt ist. Signalwörter, z.B. „yesterday", „now" „last week", helfen dir dabei, die richtige Zeit anzuwenden. Du kannst dazu noch einmal alle Regeln in der Grammatik ab Seite 86 nachlesen.*

a) I <u>felt</u> very sick yesterday, so I went to bed early and now <u>I'm feeling/I feel</u> much better.

b) In 1982, my brother <u>was</u> born.

c) I <u>am going to move</u>/I <u>am moving</u> to Australia in October. I can't stand the English weather any longer.

d) My aunt <u>gave</u> me this book for my birthday last week.

Aufgabe 24

a) <u>Do you have</u> tickets for the Rihanna concert?

b) No, I'm sorry. We <u>sold</u> the last one yesterday.

c) What a pity! But what about the open air festival which <u>takes place</u> in August?

d) Yes, we <u>still have</u> tickets for the festival.

Aufgabe 25

1	2	3	4
C	A	D	B

Aufgabe 26

✏ **Hinweis:** *Adverbien beschreiben u. a., auf welche Art und Weise etwas geschieht.*

a) gladly

b) easily

c) well

d) closely

Aufgabe 27

✏ **Hinweis:** *Die Signalwörter für die Verwendung des Simple present findest du auf Seite 86 f. in der Grammatik. Beachte bei der Bildung des Simple present den Merksatz: „He, she, it – ‚s' muss mit!"*

a) Mum <u>always</u> **wakes** me up in the morning.

b) Sally <u>often</u> **goes** hiking at the weekends.

c) <u>Every year</u>, Mr Jones **spends** his holidays in Ireland.

d) <u>On Mondays</u>, Jane **is** <u>always</u> late for school. The rest of the week she <u>usually</u> **arrives** on time.

e) Lisa <u>never</u> **does** her homework properly.

Aufgabe 28

✏ **Hinweis:** *Die Regeln zur Steigerung von Adjektiven findest du auf Seite 84 f. der Grammatik.*

a) Jessica is <u>taller</u> than Jenny.

b) Jim is <u>the tallest</u> boy in our class.

c) Sara has <u>the longest</u>/(<u>long</u>) hair.

d) Michelle's hair is <u>darker</u> than Tina's.

e) Toby is <u>better</u> at playing football than Mark.

f) But Lisa is the <u>best</u> player!

Aufgabe 29

a) "This year the weather was much <u>better</u> than last year. The sun was shining almost every day.

b) Our flat was not <u>as comfortable as</u>/(comfortable) last year: the furniture was a bit old.

c) The only thing I did not enjoy was the food: in a foreign country the bread is always <u>worse</u> than in Germany.

d) The people in Spain are a lot <u>nicer</u> than people at home: they are very interested in foreign people.

e) My uncle has been thinking about moving to Spain for years because he thinks everything is <u>better</u> there."

f) "We went to Italy. The weather wasn't <u>as good as</u> in Spain. It was raining most of the time.

g) I went there with a youth group. It was <u>more exciting than</u> spending the holidays with my parents in Wales.

h) In my opinion, Italian food is the <u>best</u> in Europe.

i) That was the best holiday I've ever had and being back here is even <u>worse</u> than the rain in Italy."

Aufgabe 30

✦ **Hinweis:** *Hier musst du die fehlenden Pronomen (Fürwörter) einsetzen. Die Regeln zur Verwendung von Pronomen findest du auf Seite 75 der Grammatik.*

Mrs Brown comes into the classroom, looks out of the window and asks her class in surprise, "Whose jacket is that lying outside?" John answers, "<u>It</u> is Lisa's." "Lisa, is that true? Is that <u>your</u> jacket?" Mrs Brown asks. "Go and get <u>it</u>, please." Then Mrs Brown notices that Lisa is not in the classroom. "Where is <u>she</u> today?" "<u>I</u> think <u>she</u> is ill," says Maggie, who sounds as if she has been crying, "<u>She</u> didn't wait for <u>me</u> this morning like <u>she</u> usually does. <u>I</u> borrowed <u>her</u> jacket yesterday and <u>she</u> told me to look after <u>it</u>. But this morning, Jack and Tim took the jacket and threw <u>it</u> around. <u>I</u> couldn't catch <u>it</u>, and then <u>they</u> threw <u>it</u> out of the window." "Is that true, <u>you</u> two?" asks Mrs Brown, "Did <u>you</u> do that? Go and get the jacket immediately, give <u>it</u> back to Maggie and say sorry to <u>her</u>. <u>You</u> will stay behind after school and clean up the classroom." Jack is very angry and says, "<u>It</u> wasn't <u>me</u>!" <u>He</u> points at Tim: "<u>He</u> did it – <u>it</u> was all <u>his</u> fault!" Mrs Brown turns to the whole class and says, "All of <u>you</u> saw <u>them</u> take the jacket and throw <u>it</u> out of the window, and did any of y<u>ou</u> help Maggie? No, y<u>ou</u> didn't. <u>I</u> have decided that y<u>ou</u> will all stay behind after school and clean up the classroom. Maggie, y<u>ou</u> go to Lisa's house straight after school, return the jacket to <u>her</u> and explain what <u>we</u>/<u>they</u> did at school today. And now, everyone, please show <u>me</u> y<u>our</u> homework!"

Aufgabe 31

✏ **Hinweis:** *Die Regeln zu den Relativsätzen und zur Verwendung der Relativpronomen kannst du in der Grammatik auf Seite 83 f. nachlesen.*

a) Doesn't the pullover <u>which</u> is lying on the floor belong to you?

b) The man <u>who</u> lives next door had an accident yesterday.

c) The book <u>which</u> you lent me last week was really exciting.

d) The woman <u>who</u> is sitting next to you is my mother.

e) The train <u>which</u> arrived late was very crowded.

Aufgabe 32

✏ **Hinweis:** *Die Regeln zu den if-clauses kannst du in der Grammatik auf den Seiten 74 f. nachlesen.*

a) If I take the train, I <u>will be</u> late.

b) If you don't take an umbrella with you, you <u>will get</u> wet.

c) If I move to America, I <u>will improve</u> my English.

d) I <u>won't tell</u> you, even if you ask me a hundred times.

Aufgabe 33

a) I would like a loaf of bread, please.

b) Could you tell me the way to the next bus station?

c) I'd like to have the menu, please.

d) Do you have this pair of jeans one size bigger?

Aufgabe 34

✏ Hinweis: Die Regeln zur Wortstellung im Englischen kannst du auf Seite 86 in der Grammatik nachlesen.

a) Paul is going to visit his aunt and uncle in California.

b) They invited him to spend the summer with them.

c) Zoe is jealous that her brother is going to make a trip.

d) Zoe's aunt promises that she can visit them soon, too.

Aufgabe 35

a) Where are you/do you come from?

b) When is your birthday?

c) What's your favourite colour?

d) Do you have/Have you got any brothers and sisters?

e) Do you have/Have you got any pets?

Aufgabe 36

a) Where are you from?/Where do you live?

b) How old are you?

c) Why are you here?

d) Do you like it here?/Do you like this town?

e) Have you ever been here before?

Aufgabe 37

✏ Hinweis: Hier ist dir auf Deutsch eine Situation vorgegeben. Überlege, wie du dich korrekt auf Englisch ausdrücken würdest. Übersetze dabei nicht die deutsche Beschreibung der Situation, sondern verwende auf Englisch die direkte Rede.

a) I like Liam Hemsworth's new film/movie /
I like the new film with Liam Hemsworth.

b) Could/Can I have a coke and (a piece of) cake, please?/
I'd like/I'll have a coke and (a piece of) cake, please.

c) What do you think of/about piercings?

d) How/What about watching a film?/Why don't we watch a film?

e) You're welcome. / Don't mention it. / Not at all.

Aufgabe 38

✎ **Hinweis:** *Versuche, dich möglichst frei auf Englisch auszudrücken und nicht nur Wort für Wort zu übersetzen.*

Travel agent: Hello, how can I help you?

You: *Hello. I would like some information on bike tours in Ireland. Do you have any brochures about tours like that?*

Travel agent: When would you like to go?

You: *In the summer holidays.*

Travel agent: Would you like to rent bikes there or are you going to take your own bikes?

You: *Could you give me some information for both possibilities? I'd like to compare prices at home and then decide.*

Travel agent: No problem. Here you are. Don't hesitate to come back if you have any questions.

You: Thank you very much. Bye.

Aufgabe 39

✎ **Hinweis:** *Beachte bei der Umformung in verneinte Sätze auch die Zeitform. Die Regeln, wie du in den verschiedenen Zeiten die Verneinungsform bildest, findest du auf Seite 86 ff.*

a) The sun isn't shining outside.

b) Jessica doesn't want to buy a pair of jeans.

c) Mr Weaver didn't enjoy the film he watched yesterday.

d) Jack isn't going to visit his grandparents in Dover this summer.

e) The Smiths don't have/haven't got a new car.

f) Sara doesn't have/hasn't got a dog.

g) The weather forecast says it won't rain tomorrow.

h) I didn't do all my homework on Friday.

i) They aren't travelling around Europe.

j) Lucy doesn't like going to the cinema.

✍ **Allgemeiner Hinweis:** *In diesem Kapitel kannst du das Leseverstehen trainieren. Im Teil „Reading Comprehension" werden neben Fragen zum groben Verständnis auch Details abgefragt. Lies den Text deshalb besonders aufmerksam und nimm ihn immer wieder zur Hand, während du die zugehörigen Aufgaben bearbeitest. Verwende bei sprachlichen Unklarheiten auch das Wörterbuch.*

Reading Comprehension Test 1: Treasure hunting at the Florida Keys

Vokabelhinweise:

Z. 2 f.: *treasure hunter: Schatzjäger*

Z. 10: *dedication: Hingabe*

Z. 30: *goods: hier: Frachtgut, Waren*

Z. 37: *to remain: bleiben*

Z. 39: *to accompany: begleiten*

Z. 41 f.: *daughter-in-law: Schwiegertochter*

Z. 59: *cargo: Fracht*

Z. 63: *emerald: Smaragd (ein Edelstein)*

Z. 63: *artefacts: Artefakte – hier: von Menschen hergestellte Gegenstände*

Z. 83: *to be convinced: überzeugt sein*

Aufgabe 1

✍ **Hinweis:** *Finde zu jedem Abschnitt die passende Überschrift. Eine Auswahl an Überschriften (A–G) ist vorgegeben. Wenn du die einzelnen Textabschnitte sorgfältig durchliest, wird es dir leichtfallen, die jeweils inhaltlich passende Überschrift zu finden.*

paragraph ❶ (lines 1–12)	C
paragraph ❷ (lines 13–27)	G
paragraph ❸ (lines 28–48)	E
paragraph ❹ (lines 49–68)	D
paragraph ❺ (lines 69–80)	A
paragraph ❻ (lines 81–90)	F

Aufgabe 2

	T	F	N
a) The *Atocha* was a Spanish ship.	✓		
b) Mel Fisher and his wife Dolores had a surf shop in California.		✓	
c) Mel and Dolores married in 1953.			✓

a) The *Atocha* was a Spanish ship.

b) Mel Fisher and his wife Dolores had a surf shop in California.

c) Mel and Dolores married in 1953.

✎ **Hinweis:** *Zwar haben Mel und Dolores im Jahr 1953 geheiratet, aber diese Information steht nicht im Text.*

d) The *Atocha* was on her way to Havanna when she sank. ☐ ✓ ☐

e) The treasure is worth about 40 million dollars. ☐ ✓ ☐

f) You can also go on diving tours to the shipwreck site. ✓ ☐ ☐

Aufgabe 3

✎ **Hinweis:** *In der Aufgabe sind verschiedene Jahreszahlen angegeben. Finde im Text das Ereignis, das im jeweiligen Jahr stattfand.*

❶	❷	❸	❹	❺	❻	❼
H	B	F	D	G	C	E

Aufgabe 4

✎ **Hinweis:** *Beantworte die Fragen anhand der Informationen aus dem Text. Es reicht, wenn du in Stichworten oder kurzen Sätzen antwortest.*

a) He had a "dive shop" and gave scuba diving trainings.
   ✎ **Hinweis:** *Z. 16 ff.*

b) 5/five
   ✎ **Hinweis:** *Z. 35 f.*

c) a (Spanish) ship/a sister ship of the *Atocha*
   ✎ **Hinweis:** *Z. 46 f.*

d) to make sure the treasures were collected properly/not damaged
   ✎ **Hinweis:** *Z. 65 ff.*

e) navigational instruments, military equipment, objects of native American origin, tools, ceramics, seeds, insects
   ✎ **Hinweis:** *Z. 75 ff.*

Vokabelhinweise:

Z. 3: *annual: jährlich*

Z. 5: *scenery: Landschaft*

Z. 6: *cameleer: Kameltreiber/in*

Z. 8: *bet: Wette*

Z. 14: *to provide: (zur Verfügung) stellen*

Z. 48 f.: *Overland Telegraph Line: Telegrafenleitung, die durch ganz Australien gelegt wurde*

Z. 49 f.: *water supply infrastructure: Wasserversorgungsnetz*

Z. 58: *plant species: Pflanzenarten*

Z. 58 f.: *to pollute: verschmutzen*

Z. 72: *breeding: Zucht*

Aufgabe 1

a) Australia

✔ **Hinweis:** Z. 3

b) camel race.

✔ **Hinweis:** Z. 6 f.

c) made a bet with a friend.

✔ **Hinweis:** Z. 8 ff.

d) Australia.

✔ **Hinweis:** Z. 20 ff.

e) they can transport goods and are used to the heat.

✔ **Hinweis:** Z. 27 ff.

f) Australians spend a lot of money.

✔ **Hinweis:** Z. 61 ff.

Aufgabe 2

✔ **Hinweis:** *Im Lesetext fehlen verschiedene Sätze. Wähle für jede Lücke den passenden Satz aus und notiere den jeweiligen Buchstaben (A–G) in der Tabelle. Beachte, dass ein Satz in keine Lücke passt.*

❶	❷	❸	❹	❺	❻
E	D	A	G	C	F

Aufgabe 3

✒ **Hinweis:** *Die Aufgabe enthält mehrere Aussagen, die alle sinngemäß im Lesetext zu finden sind. Suche nun die Stellen im Text, an denen diese Information vorkommen und gib die entsprechenden Zeilen an.*

a) lines 10–12

b) lines 29/30

c) lines 32–34

d) lines 71/72

Aufgabe 4

✒ **Hinweis:** *Hier reicht es, wenn du die Fragen mit kurzen Sätzen oder Stichworten beantwortest, die du dem Text entnehmen kannst.*

a) up to 40 km
   ✒ Hinweis: Z. *30 f.*

b) He was injured by his camel and died (because of the wounds).
   ✒ Hinweis: Z. *39 ff.*

c) too many camels/eat 80 % of plant species/pollute water holes/damage water systems/they were set free
   ✒ Hinweis: Z. *53 ff.*

d) export of live camels/export of camel meat/camel milk products
   ✒ Hinweis: Z. *66 ff.*

Reading Comprehension Test 3: Is autonomous driving becoming a reality?

Vokabelhinweise:

Z. 3: *autonomous: eigenständig*

Z. 7: *driving license: Führerschein*

Z. 9: *to fail: versagen, ausfallen*

Z. 11 f.: *to be made responsible: verantwortlich gemacht werden*

Z. 15 f.: *intention: Absicht, Zweck*

Z. 17: *to increase: erhöhen*

Z. 19: *to request: hier: verlangen*

Z. 20: *measures: Maßnahmen*

Z. 29: *to improve: verbessern*

Z. 31: *to avoid: vermeiden*

Z. 40: *lane: Spur*

Z. 41: *blind spot: „toter Winkel"*

Z. 65: loss: Verlust
Z. 68: to blame sb: jmd. die Schuld geben
Z. 69: car manufacturer: Autohersteller
Z. 72: regulations: Vorschriften, Bestimmungen
Z. 81: to announce: ankündigen
Z. 89: to estimate: schätzen

Aufgabe 1

✏ **Hinweis:** *Ordne den Textabschnitten die richtige Überschrift zu. Beachte, dass drei Überschriften nicht passen und somit nicht zugeordnet werden können.*

paragraph B	paragraph C	paragraph D	paragraph E	paragraph F
7	4	6	1	3

Aufgabe 2

✏ **Hinweis:** *Notiere die Aussagen, die mit den Informationen des Lesetextes übereinstimmen.*

1. b
2. d
3. e
4. g
5. j

Aufgabe 3

✏ **Hinweis:** *Hier sind Aussagen aufgelistet, die inhaltlich alle im Text vorkommen, jedoch etwas anders formuliert sind als im Text selbst. Suche die entsprechenden Textstellen heraus und notiere, in welche(n) Zeile(n) diese stehen.*

❶	❷	❸	❹	❺
line(s) 19–22	line(s) 38–40	line(s) 50–52	line(s) 63–65	line(s) 77–80

Aufgabe 4

✒ **Hinweis:** *Hier sind Wörter vorgegeben, die im Text vorkommen. Diese Wörter können unterschiedliche Bedeutungen haben. Lies auf S. 31 jedes Wort im Satzzusammenhang und finde heraus, welche deutsche Entsprechung jeweils Sinn ergibt.*

b) Fall   c) wichtigste/wesentliche   d) warnen   e) Führung

Reading Comprehension Test 4: Kelechi Iheanacho

Vokabelhinweise:

Z. 15: *to contribute: beitragen*
Z. 22 f.: *U-21 development squad: hier: Mannschaft für unter 21-Jährige, die weiter aufgebaut werden sollen*
Z. 47 f.: *Confederation of African Football: Afrikanischer Fußballbund*
Z. 51 f.: *to suggest: hier: nahelegen, andeuten*
Z. 53: *to aspire: anstreben*
Z. 56: *devotion: Hingabe*
Z. 56: *obstacle: Hindernis*
Z. 76 f.: *to make an effort: sich anstrengen, sich bemühen*
Z. 77 f.: *deceased: verstorben*
Z. 85: *to support: unterstützen*
Z. 86: *confidence: Zuversicht*
Z. 89: *to achieve: erreichen*
Z. 91: *to focus on sth: sich auf etwas konzentrieren*

Aufgabe 1

✒ **Hinweis:** *Entscheide, ob die Aussagen richtig (True/T) oder falsch (False/F) sind bzw. ob es dazu im Text keine Informationen gibt (Not in the text/N).*

	T	F	N
a) Kelechi plays for the national football team of Nigeria and for the first team of Manchester City.	✓	☐	☐
b) Kelechi never had any doubts that he would make it to the top.	☐	✓	☐
c) Besides a Nigerian passport, Kelechi also has a British passport. ✒ **Hinweis:** *Es wird nicht erwähnt, welchen Pass Kelechi hat.*	☐	☐	✓
d) Kelechi still has family in Nigeria.	✓	☐	☐
e) It is Kelechi's dream to become team captain of Manchester City one day.	☐	☐	✓
f) Kelechi lives together with his father in Manchester.	☐	✓	☐

29

Aufgabe 2

✎ **Hinweis:** *Bringe die Fakten in die* <u>zeitlich</u> *richtige Reihenfolge. Der überzählige Satz passt inhaltlich nicht zum Lesetext.*

1. e
    ✎ **Hinweis:** *Z. 57 ff.*
2. d
    ✎ **Hinweis:** *Z. 34 ff.*
3. f
    ✎ **Hinweis:** *Z. 17 ff.*
4. c
    ✎ **Hinweis:** *Z. 17 ff.*

Aufgabe 3

✎ **Hinweis:** *Beantworte die Fragen auf Grundlage des Lesetextes. Schreibe keine langen Sätze aus dem Text ab, sondern beschränke dich auf kurze (Teil-)Sätze bzw. Stichpunkte.*

a) (in) Nigeria
    ✎ **Hinweis:** *34 ff.*
b) Most Promising Talent of the Year
    ✎ **Hinweis:** *46 ff.*
c) 18 (years old)
    ✎ **Hinweis:** *48 f.*
d) 3/three (two brothers and one sister)
    ✎ **Hinweis:** *73 ff.*
e) to be a great player
    ✎ **Hinweis:** *91 ff.*

Aufgabe 4

✎ **Hinweis:** *Finde die Stellen im Lesetext, die inhaltlich mit den Aussagen übereinstimmen. Notiere anschließend die Fundstellen durch Angabe der jeweiligen Zeilen.*

a) lines 31–33
b) lines 52–54
c) lines 67–70
d) lines 85/86
e) lines 94/95

✔ **Allgemeiner Hinweis:** *Für das gesamte Kapitel „Text Production" ist es wichtig, dass du dir die Arbeitsschritte zum Verfassen eines Aufsatzes auf Seite 37 f. genau durchliest und dementsprechend arbeitest. Wenn du nach diesen Schritten vorgehst, wird dir ein gut strukturierter Aufsatz bestimmt nicht mehr schwerfallen.*

Aufgabe 1

✔ **Hinweis:** *Hier musst du noch keinen vollständigen Text schreiben, sondern die unterstrichenen Wörter durch Attribute näher beschreiben. Mit dieser Aufgabe kannst du für deine eigenen Aufsätze trainieren.*

a) The <u>beautiful</u>/<u>small</u> house at the end of the street belongs to my parents.

b) Grandma told me to throw the <u>old</u> <u>carpet</u> away.

c) James loves sitting in his room and listening to <u>loud</u> <u>music</u>.

d) Take off your <u>dirty</u> <u>shoes</u>!

e) I live in a <u>small</u>/<u>beautiful</u> <u>village</u>.

f) I got a <u>dark</u> <u>blue</u> coat for my birthday.

g) We travelled a lot during our <u>summer</u> <u>holidays</u>.

Aufgabe 2

✔ **Hinweis:** *Konjunktionen helfen dir, Sätze elegant zu verknüpfen und nicht nur aneinander zu reihen. Es ist hilfreich, wenn du sie mit Beispielsätzen in deine Vokabelkartei aufnimmst. Zur deutschen Entsprechung der englischen Konjunktionen vergleiche die Kurzgrammatik auf S. 78 f.*

a) I took an umbrella with me this morning <u>because</u> it was raining.

b) <u>When</u>/<u>As soon as</u> I'm 18 years old I will leave home.

c) I'd love to visit New York, <u>but</u> I don't have enough money.

d) Jack moved to another town <u>in order to</u> become independent.

e) Clara washes the dishes <u>while</u> she's talking to her best friend on the phone.

Aufgabe 3

Hinweis: Hier musst du noch keinen zusammenhängenden Text schreiben, sondern du kannst zunächst einmal üben, ein Bild zu beschreiben. Dazu musst du dir das Bild genau ansehen, um auch detaillierte Fragen beantworten zu können. Verwende die ing-Form, um zu beschreiben, was gerade geschieht.

a) It's on the coast of an island.

b) Behind the boat, there is a beach and a house. You can also see some people standing behind the boat.

c) A man with a child is standing in front of the boat.

d) He is standing in the water and looking down. He is probably holding the child's hand.

Aufgabe 4

a) The man is playing some musical instruments.

b) The man is standing in front of a shop in a town.

c) He is playing the guitar, a drum set and a harmonica.

d) There are some children standing behind the man. They are enjoying the music. One little girl is clapping her hands.

e) The man is wearing socks with the Union Jack on them. That is the British flag, so either he is from Great Britain or he just likes the socks.

Aufgabe 5

Hinweis: Hier musst du nicht mehr nur beschreiben, sondern einen kurzen Text verfassen. Natürlich kannst du die Antworten aus Aufgabe 4 als Basis für den Text nehmen.

Beispiellösung:

When I was walking along the high street yesterday, all of a sudden I saw a lot of people and heard some fantastic music. It was a man who was playing a drum set, a guitar and a harmonica all on his own. He looked very funny because he was carrying the drum set on his back. All the people who were listening enjoyed his music very much.

(68 words)

Aufgabe 6

✎ **Hinweis:** *In den vorgegeben Bildern wird eine kurze Geschichte erzählt. Fasse diese in Worte.*

Beispiellösung:

At tea time Mr Smith wanted to have some biscuits. He took the biscuit box out of the cupboard – but it was empty. Mr Smith had a suspicion: He grabbed his cat by the neck and showed it the empty box. Mr Smith said angrily: "You're a naughty, naughty cat. You should feel ashamed that you've eaten my biscuits!" The poor cat did not react, so Mr Smith let it go to tell his wife that the biscuits were gone. Mrs Smith was in the kitchen to prepare some tea and biscuits. When Mr Smith saw her with the biscuit plate, he realized that his wife had emptied the biscuit box and not their cat! This made Mr Smith feel guilty, so he apologised to the cat for his bad behaviour with a very yummy cake.   *(136 words)*

Aufgabe 7

✎ **Hinweis:** *Die Beispiellösung ist etwas länger als die vorgegebene Wortzahl, um dir Ideen für deine eigene Geschichte zu geben.*

Beispiellösung:

On Saturday evening, Jenny got on the train to meet her friends at a party. She found a nice window seat, and started to use her smartphone. She wrote to her friends: "Meet you at 6 pm at Oldham Station. Looking forward to the party :-)" Then she switched to a game app. Jenny was so busy playing her game that she didn't notice the train arriving at Oldham Station. She also didn't see her friends, who came to meet her at the station and who were waving and shouting to catch her attention: "Jenny, get off the train!"; but Jenny was so concentrated on her game that she didn't see them.

It was 8 pm when Jenny sat on a bench at Weston Station. She was very unhappy that she had missed Oldham Station and now had to wait for the next train to take her back to Oldham. She thought of her friends, having a lot of fun at the party now, and she didn't look at her smartphone again that evening.

(174 words)

Aufgabe 8

📝 **Hinweis:** *Die Wendungen auf Seite 39 ff. helfen dir, diese Aufgabe zu lösen. Es ist hilfreich, wenn du sie auswendig lernst.*

a) Dear (Aunt) Mary   Best wishes/Love

b) Dear Mrs Smith   Yours sincerely

c) Dear Luke   Best wishes/Love

d) Dear Mr O'Brien   Yours sincerely

e) Dear Grandma and Grandpa   Best wishes/Love

f) Dear Sir or Madam   Yours faithfully

g) Dear Madam   Yours faithfully

Aufgabe 9

📝 **Hinweis:** *Hier sind einige Punkte auf Deutsch vorgegeben, die dir bei der Strukturierung deiner Postkarte helfen. Auf Seite 39 f. findest du außerdem Wendungen für eine angemessene Begrüßung sowie einen angemessenen Schluss.*

7/7/…

Dear Lisa,

How are you? Hello from the USA! We're having a lot of fun here. Yesterday I went to see the musical "The Lion King" with my family in Minskoff Theatre in New York. I liked the musical because of the great music, the fantastic dancers and singers and the interesting costumes. But the tickets were quite expensive. We're going to stay in New York for one more day, then we're flying to Florida.

I'll give you a call as soon as I'm home again.

Best wishes,

(your name)   *(90 words)*

Aufgabe 10

✏ **Hinweis:** *Lies dir den Einleitungstext und die Anzeige genau durch. Die Angaben helfen dir, die Sätze sinnvoll zu ergänzen.*

(address)

(date)

Mr Tom Leary
Hotel Bellevue
63 London Road
St Albans
AL5 6 PH

Dear Mr Leary,

I am interested in working at <u>Hotel Bellevue over the summer</u>. My name is ... , I'm ... years old and I live in ... , Germany. I attend the 5th form *(entspricht der 9. Klasse)*. After finishing school I would like to work <u>in a hotel</u>. The job at your hotel would be a great opportunity to <u>gain some experience</u>.
Could you please give me some more information about the job?
How long <u>would I have to work every day</u>? How much <u>do you pay</u>?

I look forward <u>to hearing from</u> you.

Yours sincerely,

(signature)

(your name)

Aufgabe 11

Hi Sean,

How are you? Thanks a lot for your e-mail. I'm really happy because I got a job at a hotel in Cambridge for the holidays. That's great, isn't it? I will have to clean the rooms or support the staff at reception and I'll have to help out in the kitchen. I'm glad that I will earn some money. Afterwards I will still have one week left of my holidays and I would love to spend it in Dublin with you. I would like to come the last week of August and I'm looking forward to the festival which you told me about.

Best wishes,

(your name) *(108 words)*

Aufgabe 12

*✎ **Hinweis:** Für den tabellarischen Lebenslauf (Aufgabe 12 a) genügt es, wenn du in Stichpunkten antwortest. Beim Punkt „Education" gibst du deine Klassenstufe (die 9. Klasse entspricht der „5th form") und Schulart an (die Mittelschule entspricht ungefähr einer „Secondary School" in England; die Grundschule heißt „Primary School"). Gib auch besondere Fähigkeiten an, die für den Job nützlich sein könnten (z. B. good at organizing/maths/calculating/using the computer). Die Angabe deiner Hobbys rundet deinen Lebenslauf ab (z. B. travelling, reading, playing football/soccer).*

Beispiellösung Aufgabe 12 b:

(address)
(date)

Springdale Post
24 Western Street
Springdale
SP 1 5NW

ad number 45 26 78

Dear Sir or Madam,

I would like to apply for the summer job in your dry cleaning shop. My name is ... and I am ... years old. I am a pupil from Germany and I will spend my summer holiday with a host family in Springdale. I would like to earn some money for my holiday. Your ad is interesting for me because I have already worked in a dry cleaning shop in Germany. I enjoyed the work there. I am reliable, always ready to help and good at organizing. Talking to the customers would also help me to practise my English.

Can you tell me how long the working hours in your shop are?

I would really enjoy working with you and hope to hear from you soon.

Yours faithfully,

(signature)
(your name)

(133 words)

✦ **Allgemeiner Hinweis:** *Du findest hier Aufgaben zu allen Bereichen der münd-lichen Prüfung. Lies die Aufgabenstellungen genau durch, aber beachte, dass du sie in der Prüfung nicht vorgelegt bekommst, und die Aufgaben und Fragen ausschließ-lich mündlich an dich gerichtet werden. Beantworte alle Fragen möglichst ausführ-lich und begründe deine Antworten.*

Aufgabe 1

✦ **Hinweis:** *Betrachte die Zeichnung genau. An welchem Ort spielt diese Szene? Wer könnten die beiden Personen sein? Beachte unbedingt auch die Aussage unter-halb der Zeichnung: Welche der beiden gezeigten Personen stellt diese Frage? Ist diese Aussage realistisch oder möchte der Zeichner mit einer übertriebenen Aussage auf humorvolle Art Kritik am Verhalten mancher Leute üben?*

Beispiellösungen:

Scene description: There's a boy in a library. He's pointing at a book and asking the assistant a strange question.

a) I don't think the librarian understands what the boy wants. She is probably surprised by the boy's strange question because you can't print out the con-tents of a book. Normally, you can only print out a text that is on a computer. In a library, you can read a book, take notes or copy some pages on a photo-copier. Or, of course, you can borrow the book. These are the things the librar-ian would expect the boy to do with the book.

b) The boy doesn't seem to have any experience with books which are not in an electronic format but printed on paper.

c) I would tell the boy that if he wants to take some information from the book for his school paper, for example, he has to take notes or copy some of the pages.

d) The situation is rather unrealistic. Normally, pupils who go to the library to look for information are smart enough to know that you can't "print out" pages from a printed book like you can from a computer. The cartoon exagger-ates the fact that a lot of young people today are much more used to electronic media than to printed texts.

e) I prefer printed books because they offer the original reading experience. I also like to feel the pages. Printed books are simple and "work" without electronic equipment or electricity. Or:

I prefer electronic media because it is much easier to work with, and many books are available on smartphones or electronic readers. You can access books anywhere and don't have to get them at the book store or the library first. Electronic media is more interesting, e. g. because of videos, audio books, or interactive games.

Aufgabe 2

✏ **Hinweis:** *Sieh dir die Zeichnung genau an. Wie wirkt das Zimmer auf dich? Wer sind wohl die beiden Personen? Welche Beziehung könnten sie zueinander haben? Wie empfindest du die Aussage des Jungen?*

Beispiellösung:

Scene description: A teenage boy is lying on his bed in a room that is full of toys and games. A woman, probably his mother, is standing in the doorway and looking at him. The boy is telling her: "I'm bored."

a) I usually clean up my room. I don't like to have such a messy room.
   Or:
   No, I don't have so many things in my room. I also like to keep my things in order.
   Or:
   Yes, this is exactly what a cool boy's room should look like. And I have even more stuff than he does!

b) The boy's mother probably expects him to ...
   – clean up his room.
   – stop playing games all the time.
   – get out of bed and go outside to play or to exercise.
   – stop complaining about being bored because he has so many things to play with.
   – tell her what new games or toys he wants to have.

c) I think that the boy is addicted to new stuff. The thrill of having something new doesn't keep him satisfied for long, so he starts to lose interest and feels bored again. He hasn't learned to keep himself busy or deal with boredom.
   Or:
   I don't understand the boy's problem at all. It is always fun playing as many games as possible and I can never get enough of them.

Or:

Playing the same games all the time is boring. Sometimes it feels better to do sports, study or turn to a hobby. He should also spend time with his family or friends.

Or:

It looks like the boy doesn't have the really cool games to play with. So it's clear that he is bored, with that old PC, model planes and game of darts. He should get a ... instead!

d) I think that first of all the boy should stop complaining about being bored. He should go outside instead to meet friends. I think the boy needs some company. That's why he is bored.

Or:

The mother should stop buying things for her son. As long as the boy gets everything he wants, he won't learn to appreciate what he already has, which is why he is bored.

Aufgabe 3

✏ **Hinweis:** *Was fällt dir auf dem Foto auf? Achte auf die Aufschrift an der Straßenbegrenzung sowie auf die Körperhaltung und den Gesichtsausdruck der beiden jungen Frauen.*

Beispiellösung:

Scene description: There are two girls sitting on a wall. Behind the wall there is a street where cars are passing by. On the wall is a sign that reads "Do not sit or stand on wall". The girl on the left side looks like she is waiting for somebody. The girl on the right looks quite relaxed.

a) It is there because the wall is right next to the road and because the passing cars can be dangerous for pedestrians *(Fußgänger)*.

b) I don't think that the two girls are friends because they are sitting apart from each other and the girl on the left side is looking in the other direction.

c) I think she is smiling because she's thinking of something nice.

d) It is funny because the two girls are sitting on the wall although they are not allowed to.

e) It could be that they haven't read the sign. But maybe they have read it and just don't care. I don't have the impression they're sitting on the wall in order to provoke others.

39

Aufgabe 4

✏ **Hinweis:** *Betrachte das Foto. Wie alt sind die dargestellten Personen ungefähr und welche Beziehung könnten sie zueinander haben? An welchem Ort könnte das Bild aufgenommen worden sein? Womit befassen die Jugendlichen sich gerade?*

Beispiellösung:

Scene description: There are two girls and two boys sitting on the ground in a public place, probably close to a café. One of the boys has his skateboard with him. All of them are busy with their smartphones.

a) Yes, it looks like the four young people are good friends. They are sitting close to each other on the pavement. The arms of the boy and girl in the middle are touching, and the boy in the middle has also put his arm behind the boy on the right. They also have a similar style of clothing (leather jackets and denim jeans, for example), which is often typical of good friends.

b) It doesn't look like they are communicating with each other. Instead they are busy with their smartphones all by themselves. Maybe they are communicating with other people, writing messages to them, or they are using apps or playing games.

c) Yes, it is quite common to see groups of friends or families sitting together like that, with each one being busy with their smartphones. You can see them in parks, fast food restaurants or on public transport, for instance.

d) Both things are important: Meeting friends personally and staying in contact with them via messages or social networks. When I meet my friends, we can talk face to face, make jokes, laugh and have a lot of fun together. I can look at my friends' faces and see how they are feeling, or give them a hug when they are sad or worried. It is not possible to have the same kind of experience when your friends are not around in person. But I also don't want to do without staying in touch with my friends online. The advantage is that we can communicate even if we are far apart from each other or if we're busy with other things. It can also be fun to text each other and make jokes that way, or to send each other selfies of where we are at the moment.

Aufgabe 5

✏ **Hinweis:** *Sieh dir den Werbespot an. Welche Personen kommen vor? Mit welchem Problem wird der Mann konfrontiert? Wie löst er das Problem? Ist der Spot ernst oder humorvoll? An welche Zielgruppe könnte er sich richten? Wozu wird der Zuschauer (indirekt) aufgefordert?*

Beispiellösung:

Scene description: In the video you see a father carrying his little daughter to the car. When they have almost reached the car, the girl shows her father that her doll has lost a shoe. This makes the father go back over the hot sand to pick it up.

a) He desperately wants to reach his car because he is walking barefoot on hot sand and carrying his daughter as well as lots of beach equipment. He is suffering because of his heavy load, and because the hot sand and the pebbles on the car park make his feet hurt.

b) The doll has lost its shoe on the way from the beach to the car. It is now lying somewhere in the hot sand.

c) The father is unhappy because he realizes that he will have to go back to fetch the shoe, but when his daughter looks at him hopefully, he knows he has got to go back.

d) Yes, the father behaves like a superhero because first he has to walk on the hot sand to take his daughter and the beach equipment to the parking lot, and then he turns around again to go back to fetch the doll's shoe. He also doesn't leave his daughter by the car but takes her with him to get the shoe. When he turns around to go down the beach again, the wind blows up the beach towel that is wrapped around his neck, making it look like the cape of a superhero.

e) The message behind the car being "for real superheros" probably refers to parents who would do anything for their family and children. These parents are the ones who deserve this car, which is only for special people. While a superhero from a comic is a fictional character with supernatural powers (e. g. Batman, Spiderman, etc.) a "real" superhero according to this video clip is the ordinary, loving father, who does everything for his child.

Aufgabe 6

✏ **Hinweis:** *Übertrage vom Englischen ins Deutsche und umgekehrt. Denke daran, dass du nicht wortwörtlich übersetzen sollst. Manchmal musst du die Personalpronomen verändern, z. B. von „I" zu „he" oder „she".*

PHARMACIST (A WOMAN): Good morning, how can I help you?
DU ZU DEINER OMA: **Die Apothekerin fragt, wie sie uns helfen kann.**
OMA ANNELIESE: Könntest du der Apothekerin sagen, dass mir die Füße wehtun?
DU ZUR APOTHEKERIN: **My grandmother's feet hurt.**
PHARMACIST: Did your grandmother have these problems before?
DU ZU DEINER OMA: **Hattest du vorher schon mal dieses Problem?**

OMA ANNELIESE: Nein.

DU ZUR APOTHEKERIN: **No, she didn't.**

PHARMACIST: Is there any problem with her shoes?

DU ZU DEINER OMA: **Kann es an deinen Schuhen liegen?**

OMA ANNELIESE: Nein. Mit meinen Schuhen ist alles in Ordnung. Die trage ich immer.

DU ZUR APOTHEKERIN: **No, everything is OK with her shoes. She always wears them.**

OMA ANNELIESE: Kann sie mir etwas geben die Schmerzen geben?

DU ZUR APOTHEKERIN: **Could you give her something against the pain?**

PHARMACIST: Well, I think your grandmother should see a doctor.

DU ZU DEINER OMA: **Die Apothekerin meint, du solltest zum Arzt gehen.**

PHARMACIST: There is a very good doctor next door. Why don't you go there?

DU ZU DEINER OMA: **Nebenan gibt es einen guten Arzt. Wollen wir nicht dort hingehen?**

OMA ANNELIESE: Vielen Dank. Das ist eine gute Idee!

DU ZUR APOTHEKERIN: **Thank you very much. That's a good idea.**

PHARMACIST: Good luck and good bye!

DU ZU DEINER OMA: **Sie sagt, alles Gute und auf Wiedersehen.**

Aufgabe 7

✎ **Hinweis:** *Übertrage wieder vom Englischen ins Deutsche und umgekehrt. Denke an die Veränderung der Personalpronomen, wenn nötig.*

RECEPTIONIST: Good afternoon. What can I do for you?

YOU: **Guten Tag. Der Rezeptionist fragt, was er für Sie tun / wie er Ihnen helfen kann.**

GERMAN TOURIST: Schmidt, guten Tag. Ich habe eine Reservierung.

YOU: **Good afternoon. This is Mr. Schmidt./He's Mr. Schmidt.[1] He's made a reservation.**

RECEPTIONIST: Mr. Schmidt. Your reservation is from the fifteenth to the eighteenth of August. Could I have your passport and your credit card, please?

YOU: **Sie haben vom 15. bis zum 18. August reserviert. Der Rezeptionist braucht Ihren Pass und Ihre Kreditkarte.**

GERMAN TOURIST: Hier, bitte. Können Sie uns morgen um 6 Uhr aufwecken?

YOU: **Here you are. Could you please wake them up at 6 o'clock in the morning?**

RECEPTIONIST: Sure! Here's your key. Your room is number 223. Breakfast is served from 6 to 10 a.m. The breakfast room is on the first floor[2].

YOU: **Das macht er gerne. Hier ist Ihr Schlüssel. Ihr Zimmer hat die Nummer 223. Von 6 Uhr bis 10 Uhr gibt es Frühstück. Der Frühstücksraum befindet sich im Erdgeschoss.**

GERMAN TOURIST: Können wir im Hotel auch Karten für das Musical „Lion King" kaufen?

YOU: **Can Mr. Schmidt buy tickets for the musical "Lion King" at the hotel?**

RECEPTIONIST: Sorry. We don't sell theatre tickets. You can buy them at the theatres on Broadway or at the ticket office on Times Square.

YOU: **Es tut ihm leid, aber hier im Hotel werden keine Theaterkarten verkauft. Sie können sie aber in den Theatern am Broadway oder am Ticketstand am Times Square erwerben.**

GERMAN TOURIST: Danke. Auf Wiedersehen.

YOU: **Thank you. Goodbye.**

1 Übertrage deutsche Nachnamen <u>nicht</u> ins Englische
2 first floor: (in den USA:) Erdgeschoss

Aufgabe 8

✏ **Hinweis:** *Dolmetsche zwischen der deutschen Touristin und der Verkäuferin.*

ASSISTANT: Hello, can I help you?

YOU: **Die Verkäuferin fragt, ob sie Ihnen helfen kann.**

GERMAN TOURIST: Ja, bitte. Ich hätte dieses T-Shirt gerne in blau.

YOU: **Yes, please. She would like to have this T-shirt in blue, please.**

ASSISTANT: Here you are.

YOU: **Hier, bitte schön.**

GERMAN TOURIST: Wo kann ich es anprobieren?

YOU: **Where can she try it on?**

ASSISTANT: The changing rooms are over there.

YOU: **Die Umkleidekabinen sind dort drüben.**

GERMAN TOURIST: Dieses T-Shirt ist zu groß. Kann ich ein kleineres haben?

YOU: **This T-shirt is too large (for her). Could she have a smaller one, please?**

GERMAN TOURIST: *(Nach dem Anprobieren)* Jetzt passt es.

YOU: **This one fits.**

ASSISTANT: Would you like anything else?

YOU: **Brauchen Sie sonst noch etwas?/Kann sie sonst noch etwas für Sie tun?**

GERMAN TOURIST: Ich nehme auch diese beiden Postkarten. Verkaufen Sie auch Briefmarken?

YOU: **These postcards, please./She wants to have these postcards, too. Do you sell stamps?**

ASSISTANT: No, I'm sorry. You have to buy them at the post office.
YOU: **Leider nein. Die können Sie nur im Postamt kaufen.**
GERMAN TOURIST: Schade. Trotzdem danke und auf Wiedersehen.
YOU: **What a pity. Anyway, thanks for your help. Goodbye.**

Aufgabe 9

✏ **Hinweis:** *Verbinde die Stichpunkte zu einem kleinen Vortrag. Achte darauf, dass du alle vorgegebenen Stichpunkte verwendest und dass dein Vortrag einen roten Faden hat.*

Telling about a trip

Last August my friend and his parents went on a holiday to England, where they went on a bike tour. They stayed in England for two weeks. They rented the bikes in Bristol. There they started the tour along the coast. They wanted to go camping as well, but they weren't able to because it was too cold. So they stayed in hotels instead. The weather was bad: They had only two sunny days and a lot of rain instead. In the end, my friend's bike was stolen at the train station. My friend was happy when the holiday was over.

Aufgabe 10

✏ **Hinweis:** *Bilde anhand der Stichpunkte Fragen und Antworten für das Verkaufsgespräch. Achte auch hier wieder darauf, dass dein Gespräch logisch aufgebaut ist.*

PRÜFER: Hello, how can I help you?
SCHÜLER: Are there still tickets for "Star Wars" available?
PRÜFER: Yes, there are. How many would you like to have?
SCHÜLER: Three, please.
PRÜFER: The tickets for the back rows are £ 6 each, the tickets for the front rows
  £ 4. Which tickets would you like to have?
SCHÜLER: We would like to have the front row tickets for £ 4, please.
PRÜFER: Here you are. That's £ 12. Is there anything else I can do for you?
SCHÜLER: Yes, please. At what time does the film start?
PRÜFER: The film starts at 7 o'clock. That's in 20 minutes.
SCHÜLER: Where can we buy some popcorn and a coke?
PRÜFER: You can buy them at the bar over there. If you want to buy a film poster,
  you can get it here at the ticket counter. Do you want one?
SCHÜLER: No thanks, bye.

Hinweis: *Verbinde die Stichpunkte zu einem kurzen Dialog. Achte darauf, dass du alle vorgegebenen Stichpunkte verwendest und dass dein Dialog sinnvoll ist.*

YOU: Hi, where are you from?

BOY: Hi there, nice to meet you, our group is from Manchester, England.

YOU: Are you here on a holiday?

BOY: No, we're not. We are here for a student exchange with a German school.

YOU: Do you like the music?

BOY: Yeah, it's great!

YOU: You know what? I was about to go for a drink, do you want something?

BOY: Yes, I'd like a coke, please.

YOU: Sure, I'll get it.

BOY: By the way, what's your name? I'm Dylan.

YOU: I'm … Just a moment, I'll be right back.

Hinweis: *Denke daran, dein Referat klar zu gliedern:*

Einleitung: *Gib an, worüber du dein Referat hältst und warum du dieses Thema gewählt hast. Zur Veranschaulichung kannst du z. B. ein Harry-Potter-Buch, ein Filmplakat oder ein Foto von J. K. Rowling mitbringen.*

Hauptteil: *Unterteile dein Referat in Sinnabschnitte, z. B. das Leben von J. K. Rowling vor dem Erfolg, der Erfolg der Harry-Potter-Bücher, das Leben von J. K. Rowling mit dem Erfolg. Dein Referat sollte alle wichtigen Informationen zur Autorin enthalten. Die Angaben müssen richtig sein. Informiere dich deshalb gründlich, z. B. im Internet.*

Schluss: *Am Ende des Referats kannst du nochmals deine eigene Meinung darlegen. Der Schluss kann auch ein Fazit/eine Zusammenfassung des Gesagten in einem Satz enthalten.*

In der Prüfung könnten folgende Fragen gestellt werden: "Why do you think so many people around the world are Harry Potter fans? What do you like about J. K. Rowling? You like reading. What other hobbies do you have?"

Like many people, I am a great fan of Harry Potter. I have read all Harry Potter books and seen the films. Today I would like to tell you a few things about the woman who invented Harry Potter, the British author Joanne Kathleen Rowling. Better known as J. K. Rowling, she was born in Yate, England, in 1965. She grew up in Chepstow in Wales and then went to study French at Exeter University. As a student, she also spent a year in Paris. Later, J. K. Rowling moved to London to work for the human rights organization[1] Amnesty International.

J. K. Rowling had the idea of Harry Potter while she was on a train from Manchester to London in 1990. She could only write in her free time. J. K. Rowling studied to become a teacher and moved to Portugal, where she taught English. She got married there and had a baby. But later she had to raise[2] the child by herself. Sometimes she was only able to write the Harry Potter book when her little daughter was sleeping.

Before publishing[3] the first book, J. K. Rowling had very little money. While she was still studying to become a teacher, she and her baby had to live on 70 pounds a week.

"Harry Potter and the Philosopher's Stone" was finally published in 1997 and was a great success[4]. Before that, lots of children had only been interested in television or computer games, but then they started to read again. However, it was not just children who liked Harry Potter – their parents did, too. J. K. Rowling became one of the best-selling authors in the world. The seventh and final book, "Harry Potter and the Deathly Hallows", was sold 11 million times in the first day after the sales[5] started. It is the "fastest selling book in history". You can buy Harry Potter books in about 200 countries and in 65 languages. The Harry Potter films have also been very successful.

J. K. Rowling has also won many international prizes for her books and has become very rich – but she has remained an uncomplicated and nice person!

(358 words)

1   human rights organization: Menschenrechtsorganisation
2   (to) raise: aufziehen
3   (to) publish: veröffentlichen
4   success: Erfolg
5   sale: Verkauf

Aufgabe 13

✎ **Hinweis:** *Denke daran, dein Referat klar zu gliedern:*

Einleitung: *Nenne das Thema deines Referates und begründe, warum du es gewählt hast.*

Hauptteil: *Wenn du über einen Urlaub berichtest, kannst du der Reihe nach erzählen, was passiert ist, oder du suchst dir nur bestimmte wichtige Ereignisse aus, von denen du berichtest. Wenn du Fachbegriffe verwendest, oder die Namen bestimmter Attraktionen nennst, solltest du erklären, was sie bedeuten, bzw. was es dort zu sehen gibt. Bringe zur Veranschaulichung Fotos oder Souvenirs mit oder erstelle ein Plakat.*

Schluss: *Fasse den Inhalt deines Referats kurz zusammen oder finde einen Schluss, der das Referat abrundet.*
In der Prüfung könnten folgende Fragen gestellt werden: "What activity did you like best and why? What sights did you see? What was your best memory?"

I would like to tell you about the fantastic holiday I spent with my family this summer. My parents, my sister and I spent three weeks in Florida, which is a very exciting place to go to.

In the middle of August, we flew to Miami. Because we had to change planes in Chicago, the trip took 15 hours and we were very tired when we arrived. My parents rented[1] a car at the airport and we drove to a holiday flat[2] in Fort Lauderdale, where we all fell into bed. The next day, we all wanted to go to the beach first, so we drove to Miami Beach where we had a beach picnic for lunch. But it was too hot! It was 36 to 38 degrees and you had to wear sandals when walking in the sand because it was so hot! But my sister and I ran into the sea and it was great!

For the first week we stayed in Fort Lauderdale. We went to the beach and sometimes we went on a trip. In Miami we saw the Seaquarium, where they do shows with killer whales and dolphins. We also went to a parrot park, where we saw thousands of colourful birds. Some birds even sat down on the visitors and we took a lot of photos there. Once, we also went to a big flea market in Fort Lauderdale, where we stayed for the whole afternoon. My sister and I bought some souvenirs there.

In the second week, we first drove to Orlando, which is in the middle of Florida, where we stayed in a motel for a couple of days. We went to different fun parks like Disney World and the MGM Studios. But I liked the Epcot Center best. It is a big park where you can go on different rides but also see a lot of interesting films or shows about other cultures, nature or animals. The next time I go to Florida, I will go to the Epcot Center again for sure! After Orlando, we drove to the Lyndon B. Johnson Space Center, where we lost my sister and had to look for her for two hours before we found her. So we didn't see all of the spaceships. We then spent a few more days at the beach.

At the end of our holiday, my father wanted to drive to Key West. We drove for a whole day, and at the end of the trip we crossed a lot of bridges which go right over the ocean. In Key West we went to the spot which is the southernmost tip[3] of the USA. We bought more souvenirs and went to see a museum about treasure hunting[4] in the sea. We also saw the house of Ernest Hemingway, the famous author.

We were all sad when we had to drive back to the airport in Miami. But my parents promised that we would travel to Florida again soon!

1 (to) rent: mieten
2 flat: Apartment
3 southernmost tip: das südlichste Ende
4 treasure hunting: Schatzsuchen

Aufgabe 14

a) Keira Knightley acted in *Star Wars Episode I*, *Bend It Like Beckham* and *Pirates of the Caribbean*, for example.
b) *(Your personal answer)* I have seen all the *Pirates of the Caribbean* films. I think they are great!
c) Yes, Keira earned money as a model (on television and working for Chanel).
d) *(Your personal answer)* I think she is a good and successful actress and a beautiful woman.

Aufgabe 15

1. Men started to wear skirts again in the second half of the 20th century[1].
2. There are only a few expensive brands, so it is not possible to buy men's skirts in every clothing store. *(Or your personal answer from your own shopping experience.)*
3. *(Your answer)* I have never seen a man in my town wearing a men's skirt, but I once saw a photo in a magazine of a famous star wearing a skirt. I think it was David Beckham.
4. *(Your answer)* In my opinion men should wear trousers when they go to work. But in their free time they could wear a skirt. I'm sure that a man who wears a skirt at the disco or in a pub would get a lot of attention!

1 20th century: das 20. Jahrhundert (die Jahre von 1901 bis 2000)

A Listening

Allgemeiner Hinweis: *Die folgenden Dialoge hörst du je zweimal. Achte genau auf die Anweisungen. Versuche, die Aufgaben selbstständig zu lösen und sieh die Lösungen erst nach Bearbeitung der Aufgaben an.*

Part 1

1   JENNY: Hello. Um. ... Heathrow Airport, please.
TAXI DRIVER: Heathrow? OK. Where are you flying to?
JENNY: Sorry?
TAXI DRIVER: Which terminal is it?
5   JENNY: It's terminal ... um ... wait a second ... one, I think. To Munich.
TAXI DRIVER: OK. Which airline did you say?
JENNY: British Airways. At 11.30.
TAXI DRIVER: British Airways? Ah, that's terminal 5.
JENNY: Really?
10   TAXI DRIVER: Yeah, all British Airways flights go from there.
JENNY: Let me check. Um. Yeah, yeah. You're right.
(Taxi hält an.)
TAXI DRIVER: OK. Here we are. That's £ 23.50, please.
JENNY: Thank you.
15   TAXI DRIVER: Oh, thanks. Do you need any help with your bags?
JENNY: That'd be lovely. They're quite heavy.
TAXI DRIVER: OK. You grab a trolley and I'll get everything out of the boot.
JENNY: Thanks.
TAXI DRIVER: There you are. When did you say your flight was?
20   JENNY: 11.30.
TAXI DRIVER: Oh, you'd better hurry then. It's quarter to eleven already.
JENNY: Really? 10.45. Oh no!

1. 11.30
   Hinweis: *Z. 7*
2. 5
   Hinweis: *Z. 8*
3. £ 23.50
   Hinweis: *Z. 13*

4. 10.45
/ Hinweis: *Z. 22*

Part 2

1 JENNY: Hello.
MAN FROM BA: Hello there.
JENNY: I'm booked on the 11.30 flight to Munich but I haven't been able to check in yet.
5 MAN FROM BA: That's OK. Can I have your passport, please? Thanks. How many items of luggage are you checking in? Two?
JENNY: No, just this big suitcase.
MAN FROM BA: OK. And that bag? Is that your hand luggage?
JENNY: That's right. I'm not too late, am I?
10 MAN FROM BA: No, no. Can you put the suitcase on the scales, please?
JENNY: It's quite heavy, but I hope it's not ... too heavy.
MAN FROM BA: Hmm ... seventeen kilos. That's fine. The weight limit is 23.
JENNY: Oh, good. Do you think I could have a window seat?
MAN FROM BA: Let me have a look. Um. No, I'm afraid that's not going to work.
15   And there are no aisle seats left either.
JENNY: Oh, OK.
MAN FROM BA: Sorry about that. So, that's 16 B.
JENNY: 16 B. OK. Thanks.
MAN FROM BA: Boarding begins at five past eleven so you've got 10 minutes.
20 JENNY: Great. Thanks.
MAN FROM BA: Gate 15.
JENNY: OK. Is that far to walk?
MAN FROM BA: No, no, it's very close. You can see it from here.

1. a bag and a suitcase.
/ Hinweis: *Z. 7–9*

2. 17 kilos.
/ Hinweis: *Z. 12*

3. a middle seat.
/ Hinweis: *Z. 13–15*

Part 3

1 VOICE: Good morning, ladies and gentlemen. This is an important announcement
for passengers checked in on flight BA 942 to Munich. This flight is scheduled
to leave at 11.30. Because of a problem we are having with the onboard computer system there will be a short delay. We apologise for this situation. You
5 will understand that our engineers are doing everything they can to make sure
the flight leaves as soon as possible. We would ask all passengers to stay near
the gate and wait for further announcements. We hope to give you an update
in the next ten to fifteen minutes. Once again, we apologise for the delay.

1. This is an important announcement for passengers ~~booked~~ in on flight BA 942
   to Munich.
   Hinweis: Z. 2 *(checked in)*

2. Because of a problem we are having with the onboard computer system there
   will be a ~~small~~ delay.
   Hinweis: Z. 4 *(short)*

3. You will understand that our ~~pilots~~ are doing everything they can to make sure
   the flight leaves as soon as possible.
   Hinweis: Z. 5 *(engineers)*

4. We would ask all passengers to ~~sit~~ near the gate and wait for further announcements.
   Hinweis: Z. 6 *(stay)*

Part 4

1 YOUNG WOMAN: Hey, are you also waiting for the flight to Munich?
JENNY: Yeah.
YOUNG WOMAN: Have you been on holiday here?
JENNY: No, no. I was doing a language course, in Brighton.
5 YOUNG WOMAN: Oh, Brighton! I know Brighton well. And did you enjoy it?
JENNY: Yeah, it was excellent. And I was staying with a family there. They were
great, too.
YOUNG WOMAN: Oh, so it was quite intensive then. One week, did you say?
JENNY: No, two weeks. And yesterday I was in London, in Brixton ...
10 YOUNG WOMAN: Brixton. OK.
JENNY: ... visiting some friends and doing some shopping.
YOUNG WOMAN: Lovely.
JENNY: And last night we all went to a musical ...
YOUNG WOMAN: OK.

₁₅ JENNY: And then in the evening when we got back I forgot to set my alarm clock …
YOUNG WOMAN: Oh dear.
JENNY: … and this morning I missed the train.
YOUNG WOMAN: Oh no.
JENNY: So I had no time for breakfast and had to get a taxi instead.
₂₀ YOUNG WOMAN: Well, you made it.
JENNY: Yeah. The taxi was expensive, but the driver was really friendly.
(Pause)
YOUNG WOMAN: Look, would you like a cup of coffee?
JENNY: That's a good idea. I need to eat something as well.
₂₅ YOUNG WOMAN: Shall we go over there to that café?
(Jingle)
JENNY: Wait a second. That could be for us.
YOUNG WOMAN: Oh no. Not another delay!
VOICE: Thank you for being so patient, ladies and gentlemen. BA 942 to Munich
₃₀ is now ready for boarding. Please have your passport *(fade out)* and boarding
card ready when you come forward to the gate. Thank you again. We wish you
a pleasant flight.

1. False
   Hinweis: Z. 4 *("I was doing a language course …")*

2. False
   Hinweis: Z. 6 *("… I was staying with a family there.")*

3. True
   Hinweis: Z. 9

4. False
   Hinweis: Z. 13 *("… we all went to a musical.")*

5. False
   Hinweis: Z. 15 *("… in the evening … I forgot to set my alarm clock.")*

6. True
   Hinweis: Z. 19

7. True
   Hinweis: Z. 21

8. True
   Hinweis: Z. 25 ff.

B Use of English

Hinweis: *Diesen Prüfungsteil musst du <u>ohne</u> das Wörterbuch bearbeiten. Anhand der folgenden Aufgaben werden dein Wortschatz, deine Ausdrucksfähigkeit in kommunikativen Situationen sowie deine Grammatik-Kenntnisse beurteilt. Falls du dir in der Grammatik einmal unsicher sein solltest, kannst du das jeweilige Thema in der Kurzgrammatik dieses Trainingsbuches (ab S. 77) nachschlagen.*

Aufgabe 1

Every day I <u>turn on</u> my computer. Sometimes I <u>need</u> it for my homework because we often have to <u>write</u> texts. Once I lost an important text so now I always <u>save</u> everything immediately. There are also a lot of photos on my computer. I <u>send</u> the nicest ones to my friends.

Aufgabe 2

a) menu   b) bill

c) kitchen   d) knife

Aufgabe 3

Hinweis: *Zu Hause kannst du dir die einzelnen Wörter laut vorsprechen, dann fallen dir Gemeinsamkeiten in der Aussprache leichter auf.*

a) there – pair

b) own – stone

c) said – bread

d) why – pie

Aufgabe 4

Hinweis: *Hier sollst du die richtige Steigerungsform des jeweiligen Adjektivs einsetzen. Zur Steigerung der Adjektive siehe S. 88 f. deiner Kurzgrammatik.*

London is the <u>biggest</u> city in England. The London Underground is the <u>oldest</u> underground system in the world. People use it because it is <u>faster</u> than the buses. Taking a taxi is <u>more expensive</u> than using public transport. One of the <u>best</u> ways to get around the centre of London is on foot.

Aufgabe 5

🖊 **Hinweis:** *Wähle jeweils das passende Verb aus und setze es in die simple past-Form.*
🖊 *Zu Formen und Verwendung des simple past siehe S. 92 in deiner Kurzgrammatik.*

Yesterday Susan <u>met</u> her friend Beth in town. First the girls <u>went</u> to a café and <u>had</u> a milkshake. Then they <u>did</u> some shopping. They <u>spent</u> an hour in a clothes shop but they <u>didn't buy</u> anything. Later they <u>watched</u> an interesting film at the cinema.

Aufgabe 6

🖊 **Hinweis:** *Hier musst du jeweils die richtige Antwort oder Reaktion auf eine Frage*
🖊 *oder Aussage ankreuzen.*

a) Good idea.

b) You're welcome. *(Bitte./Gern geschehen.)*

c) Fine, thanks.

C Reading

🖊 **Allgemeiner Hinweis:** *In diesem Prüfungsteil darfst du ein zweisprachiges Wörter-*
🖊 *buch benutzen.*

Aufgabe 1

lines 1–10	lines 11–25	lines 26–37	lines 38–46	lines 47–58	lines 59–69	lines 70–81
D	H	A	C	B	F	G

Aufgabe 2

🖊 **Hinweis:** *Markiere im Text die Sätze, die das Gleiche bedeuten wie die angegebenen*
🖊 *Sätze, und schreibe sie auf.*

a) A movie has been made about him.
🖊 **Hinweis:** *Z. 7 f*

b) (Today) around 700 million people have Facebook accounts.
   oder: (He started) a company that millions of people all over the world use.
🖊 **Hinweis:** *Z. 26 f. und Z. 5 ff.*

c) You can contact individuals and groups easily.
🖊 **Hinweis:** *Z. 39 f.*

d) Of course there are some users who aren't worried about protecting their data.
oder:
They don't mind if everyone can see them and read about them.
✎ Hinweis: *Z. 62 ff. und S. Z. 64 ff.*

Aufgabe 3

✎ **Hinweis:** *Lies den Text noch einmal durch und beantworte die Fragen in Stichpunk-*
✎ *ten oder kurzen Sätzen.*

a) (near) New York (City)
✎　Hinweis: *Z. 15 f.*

b) ZuckNet
✎　Hinweis: *Z. 19*

c) in 2003
✎　Hinweis: *Z. 22*

d) Facebook passes on data to other companies.
✎　Hinweis: *Z. 56 f.*
　oder:
　(through) advertisements/advertising
✎　Hinweis: *Z. 50–53*

e) telephone
　face-to-face conversation
　handwritten letter(s)
✎　Hinweis: *Z. 75 ff. (Im Text sind drei Möglichkeiten erwähnt, von denen du zwei*
✎　*angeben musst.)*

D Text Production

✎ **Allgemeiner Hinweis:** *Auch in diesem Prüfungsteil darfst du ein zweisprachiges*
✎ *Wörterbuch verwenden. Entscheide dich bei der Bearbeitung entweder für die E-*
✎ *mail oder für die Bildergeschichte.*

1. Correspondence: E-Mail

✎ **Hinweis:** *In der Aufgabenstellung findest du Vorgaben zum Inhalt der E-mail. Baue*
✎ *alle Vorgaben in deinen Text ein. Hier und da sollst du eigene Ideen hinzufügen, z. B.*
✎ *über den Fundort des Handys. Da du einem Freund/einer Urlaubsbekanntschaft*
✎ *schreibst, kannst du Umgangssprache verwenden.*

Hi Luca,

How are you? I hope you are fine. My family and I returned from Italy yesterday. Guess what I found on the day you left: your mobile phone! When I went to the beach I saw it on the bench that we had sat on. I could send you the mobile by post. Is that OK with you or do you have another idea?

I'm sorry that you had to go home one week before I did. It was pretty boring after that. How was your trip home? I hope you had a good journey.

After you left I spent most of the time with my family. We visited some of the nearby towns and went shopping. I also went jogging every day.

I attached the photos I took on your last day. I think they are quite funny. Please also send me the photos that you have taken.

I hope to hear from you soon!

Bye,

Emily

2. Picture-based Writing:

Hinweis: *Bevor du mit dem Schreiben beginnst, solltest du die Abbildungen genau betrachten. Verwende die inhaltlichen Vorgaben, die du in den Sprechblasen findest, in deinem Text und arbeite den Hauptteil sowie das Ende der Geschichte aus.*

… Anna was trying on the dress when Julia suddenly saw a wallet. It was under the bench of the changing room. Julia looked inside the wallet and found a card with the name "David Brown" on it and a mobile phone number. At the same time Anna saw the price tag of the dress. It cost 99 pounds! Anna didn't have so much money. So she had to put back the dress. Anna looked at other dresses that cost less. But she didn't like any of them. In the meantime, Julia called Mr Brown. She said: "Hello, is that Mr Brown? I found your wallet!" He was very happy and answered: "Let's meet at the café at 3 pm." When Anna and Julia met Mr Brown to give him his wallet, he gave each girl 20 pounds. The girls were very excited. Julia lent[1] Anna her 20 pounds. With the extra money Anna could buy the nice dress after all.

1 to lend: (ver)leihen

Notenschlüssel

Notenstufen	1	2	3	4	5	6
Punkte	72–64	63,5–52	51,5–39	38,5–25	24,5–12	11,5–0

A Listening

Allgemeiner Hinweis: *Die Hörtexte werden in der Prüfung auf CD dargeboten. Die Aufnahmen werden insgesamt zweimal ohne zusätzliche Erklärungen oder Unterbrechungen abgespielt. Lies dir die Aufgaben vor dem Hören genau durch. Während des Hörens, bzw. im Anschluss daran, bearbeitest du die zugehörigen Aufgaben. Bei den Aufgaben (Tasks) 1 und 3 darfst du jeweils nur <u>ein</u> Kästchen pro Reihe ankreuzen. Markierst du mehrere Kästchen, bekommst du keinen Punkt für die jeweilige Teilaufgabe.*

Part 1

1 RECEPTIONIST: Hi, can I help you?

PAUL: Hi, yeah, we wanted to know if we can book a boat trip.

ALISON: And maybe you could recommend one to us.

RECEPTIONIST: Sure. A lot of our guests do this one. *(Gets a brochure and opens it.)*

5 ALISON: Oh, dolphins!

RECEPTIONIST: Yeah. This is a four-hour trip to watch the wild dolphins and their babies.

PAUL: Great, and can we go in the water, too?

RECEPTIONIST: Yeah, you can go snorkeling but not where the dolphins are, of

10 course.

PAUL: Yeah, OK. And are there trips every day?

RECEPTIONIST: Yeah, every day, leaving at 9 o'clock and getting back at around 1.30.

ALISON: OK. And how much does it cost?

15 RECEPTIONIST: Well, it's usually $ 95 over the phone and 90 over the internet, but we can do it for you for 85.

PAUL: OK.

ALISON: And do we have to book in advance?

RECEPTIONIST: You do, I'm afraid. The day before. Tomorrow's trip is almost full

20 but there's still space on Friday.

PAUL: OK, we'll think about it and let you know.

RECEPTIONIST: OK.

PAUL AND ALISON: Thanks.

Vokabelhinweise: *Z. 3: to recommend: empfehlen; Z. 9: to snorkel: schnorcheln; Z. 18: in advance: im Voraus*

1. watch dolphins.
   ✍ **Hinweis:** *Z. 6 f.*

2. snorkeling.
   ✍ **Hinweis:** *Z. 9*

3. 9 to 1.30.
   ✍ **Hinweis:** *Z. 12 f.*

4. $ 85.
   ✍ **Hinweis:** *Z. 16*

5. on Friday.
   ✍ **Hinweis:** *Z. 20*

Part 2

1 TV MAN: OK, and let's have a look at the weather coming up over the next three
  days. Today it's going to be partly cloudy with temperatures steady at around
  75 Fahrenheit. The chance of rain is about 20 % and the easterly winds are
  going to be between 15 to 20 mph.

5 Tomorrow, Thursday, it's going to feel quite breezy, too, with easterly winds
  between 25 to 30 mph. There's going to be a mix of sunshine and clouds. The
  chance of rain will be around 30 %, but all in all it'll feel warm out there with
  temperatures reaching a high of 85.

  Moving on to Friday now. Friday's going to start clear and bright but with

10 easterly winds reaching 35 mph there's a 50 % chance of rain by the late afternoon. Temperatures are going to climb to a maximum of 95 and it's going to
  feel pretty humid, too.

  OK, so after the break, we'll be welcoming a special guest because *(fade begins
  here)* City Manager Billy Wardlow will be here to talk about the new parking

15 regulations that are being introduced next year and what they're going to mean.

Vokabelhinweise:
Z. 2: partly cloudy: teilweise bewölkt; steady: gleichbleibend (konstant)
Z. 5: breezy: windig

	Temperature in Fahrenheit (°F)	Chance of rain in percent (%)	Winds in miles per hour (mph)
Today	75	20	15–20
Thursday	85	30	25–30
Friday	95	50	35

Hinweis: *In den USA wird v. a. die Fahrenheit-Skala verwendet, um Temperaturen anzugeben: 75° Fahrenheit (Z. 3) = 23,9 °C, 85° Fahrenheit (Z. 8) = 29,4 °C, 95° Fahrenheit (Z. 11) = 35 °C.*
In einigen englischsprachigen Ländern wird die Einheit mph (miles per hour) verwendet, um Geschwindigkeiten anzugeben: 35 mph (Z. 10) entsprechen rund 56 km/h.
Die richtigen Lösungen findest du in folgenden Abschnitten: Today (Z. 2–4), Thursday (Z. 5–8), Friday (Z. 9–12)

Part 3

1 RECEPTIONIST: Hello there.

PAUL/ALISON: Hi.

RECEPTIONIST: Made up your mind about the boat trip yet?

PAUL: Yeah, we'd like to book for tomorrow if that's possible.

5 RECEPTIONIST: Oh, I'm sorry but tomorrow's trip's been cancelled because of the bad weather. How about Saturday?

ALISON: We're leaving on Saturday. Tomorrow's our last day.

RECEPTIONIST: Have you thought about going to *SeaWorld*?

PAUL: But that's quite a long way, isn't it?

10 RECEPTIONIST: Yeah, you're right, about 140 miles, so about 2 hours by car.

ALISON: Do you really want to be sitting in a car for four hours if we've got a 10-hour flight the next day?

PAUL: No, you're right.

ALISON: I'd rather be here tomorrow.

15 PAUL: And today? What else could we do?

RECEPTIONIST: Have you ever tried parasailing – you know, in a parachute from behind a boat?

ALISON: That sounds cool!

RECEPTIONIST: You can do it together – tandem parasailing.

20 PAUL: Locally?

RECEPTIONIST: Yes, there's a place about ten minutes on foot from here. I'll show you on the map where it is.

ALISON: Great. Then we can walk down there and check it out.

PAUL: That's a good idea.

Vokabelhinweise:

Z. 10: 140 miles: ca. 225 km
Z. 16: parachute: Fallschirm
Z. 20: locally: in der Nähe

1. False
/ **Hinweis:** Z. 5 *("tomorrow's trip's been cancelled")*

2. True
/ **Hinweis:** Z. 7

3. False
/ **Hinweis:** Z. 10

4. True
/ **Hinweis:** Z. 19

5. False
/ **Hinweis:** Z. 21 *("on foot")*

Part 4

---

1 SUNRISE: Hi, how can I help?

ALISON: Hi, I wanted to ask if we can join one of your trips today.

SUNRISE: Sure. When do you want to go?

ALISON: Well, this afternoon would be great.

5 SUNRISE: How about 2 o'clock. Or 3 o'clock?

ALISON: Two's fine. Do we need to bring anything special with us?

SUNRISE: Well the usual stuff – a towel, sunscreen and sunglasses. Oh, and your camera, of course.

ALISON: And do you need to see our passports?

10 SUNRISE: No, no.

ALISON: No identification or anything?

SUNRISE: No, just the name of the hotel where you're staying.

ALISON: OK. Um … oh yes: my boyfriend's a bit scared of heights so I wanted to know how high up we go.

15 SUNRISE: About 500 feet – but that's the maximum.

ALISON: Okay. And how long is the trip?

SUNRISE: About 45 minutes, and you're up in the air for about 10 minutes. But your boyfriend needn't worry. You'll be up there with him holding his hand!

Alison: True. I'll tell him that.

Vokabelhinweise:

Z. 7: sunscreen: Sonnencreme

Z. 11: identification: Ausweis

Z. 15: 500 feet: ca. 153 m

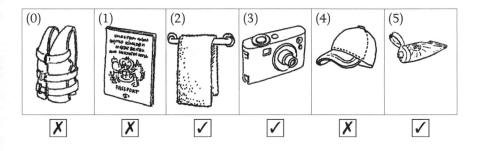

| (0) | (1) | (2) | (3) | (4) | (5) |
| ✗ | ✗ | ✓ | ✓ | ✗ | ✓ |

B Use of English

🖊 **Hinweis:** *In diesem Teil werden dein Wortschatz und deine Grammatik-Kenntnisse geprüft. Sind bei einer Aufgabe Wörter bereits vorgegeben, achte beim Einsetzen des ausgewählten Wortes in die Lücke darauf, das Wort richtig zu schreiben. Abschreibfehler führen nämlich zu Punktverlust, den du mit etwas Sorgfalt vermeiden kannst.*

Aufgabe 1

🖊 **Hinweis:** *Setze hier die passenden Wörter ein. Überlege dir, wie die einzelnen Wörter auf Deutsch heißen, denn einige dieser Namenwörter kann man auf Englisch leicht verwechseln, z. B. cloths (Tücher/Lappen) – clothes (Kleidung), counties (Grafschaften/Bezirke) – countries (Länder). Die schräg gedruckten Wörter im Text geben dir den Hinweis auf das fehlende Wort.*

Last year I travelled around the world for three <u>months</u> in *June, July and August*. I went to *Japan, India, the USA* and a lot of other <u>countries</u>. Of all the cities I saw I like New York best. When I was there I visited *the Empire State Building, the Statue of Liberty, Times Square* and many other well-known <u>sights</u>. I went to a fashion store and bought a *jacket, trousers, a shirt* and other <u>clothes</u> which are cheaper than in England. New York was full of tourists. I heard them speak *French, Chinese, Russian* and many other <u>languages</u>.

Aufgabe 2

🖊 **Hinweis:** *Hier musst du Wörter finden, die dieselbe Bedeutung haben wie die Wörter in Klammern.*

Woman: When does the show <u>finish</u> this evening?
Man: At about 10 o'clock.
Woman   <u>Maybe</u> we can have dinner somewhere afterwards.

Man:	Good idea.		
Woman:	Are there any restaurants close to the theatre?		
Man:	I don't think so. But we can <u>walk</u> somewhere.		
Woman:	No, let's <u>take</u> / <u>call</u> a taxi.		
Man:	OK.		
Woman:	And let's <u>book</u> a table.		

Aufgabe 3

/ **Hinweis:** *Hier geht es darum, die richtige Form des angegebenen Verbs einzusetzen.*
/ *Achte hier u.a. auf die grammatikalischen Zeiten (tenses) und die Signalwörter,*
/ *nach denen eine bestimmte Form verwendet werden muss.*

Signalwort	Form	Zeit	Besonderheit
at the age of ten	learned	simple past	–
when	was	simple past	–
good at	swimming	–	-*ing*-Form nach „to be good <u>at</u>"
usually	wins	simple present	Mike win<u>s</u>
next year	will have, 'll have	will future	

At the age of ten I <u>learned</u> how to surf. When I got my own board I <u>was</u> so happy. Now I'm not only good at <u>surfing</u>. I'm also a very good swimmer. Every weekend my friend Mike and I meet at a lake. Often we race against each other and Mike usually <u>wins</u>. At the moment I'm saving for a special course in Spain. I hope that I <u>'ll have</u> / <u>will have</u> enough money next year.

Aufgabe 4

/ **Hinweis:** *Ergänze hier die Sätze mit den richtigen Wörtern aus dem Kasten. Achte*
/ *dabei auf den Textzusammenhang.*

Jack and his sister Tina spent a weekend <u>in</u> London. When they got <u>to</u> the station, Jack carried his sister's suitcase <u>because</u> it was so heavy. They took the Underground to <u>their</u> aunt. She lives in a small flat all by herself and she is a great cook. Whenever she <u>has</u> guests, she likes to cook for them.

Aufgabe 5

Hinweis: *Hier musst du einen Dialog ergänzen. Mithilfe der vorgegebenen Antwor-ten kannst du die fehlenden Fragen erschließen.*

Tina:	Excuse me? <u>Can you help me?</u>
Londoner:	Yes, of course.
Tina:	<u>Is there a bus</u> / <u>Is this the bus</u> / <u>Could you tell me if there is a bus</u> / <u>Do you know if there is a bus</u> to the Tower?
Londoner:	Yes, it's bus number 15.
Tina:	How long <u>does it take</u> / <u>will it take</u> / <u>will it be</u> to get there?
Londoner:	Not long. About twenty minutes.
Tina:	How <u>much is it</u> / <u>much does it cost</u> / <u>much is the ticket?</u>
Londoner:	I'm not sure but the driver will know the price.
Tina:	<u>Do you know</u> / <u>Would you tell me</u> / <u>Could you tell me</u> if there's a bus stop nearby?
Londoner:	Yes, just around the corner.
Tina:	Thank you.
Londoner:	No worries.

C Reading Comprehension

Allgemeiner Hinweis: *Lies den Text erst einmal durch, damit du weißt, wovon er handelt. Sieh dir die Aufgaben an und suche die Stellen im Text, die dir den Hinweis auf die richtige Lösung geben.*

Vokabelhinweise:

Z. 8: *to take part in: teilnehmen an*

Z. 8 f.: *state-wide surf competition: Surf-Wettbewerb mit Teilnehmern aus den ein-zelnen Bundesstaaten der USA*

Z. 10: *passion: Leidenschaft*

Z. 13: *15-foot tiger shark: 4,5 m langer Tigerhai*

Z. 16: *to recover: sich erholen*

Z. 17: *physically: körperlich*

Z. 17: *mentally: seelisch*

Z. 17: *attitude: Einstellung*

Z. 18: *faith: Glaube*

Z. 26: *success: Erfolg*

Z. 34: *foundation: Stiftung*

Z. 35: *non-profit: gemeinnützig, nicht auf Gewinn ausgerichtet*

Z. 35: *to support: unterstützen*

Z. 35: *survivor: Überlebende(r)*

Aufgabe 1

✎ **Hinweis:** *Finde hier zu jedem Absatz die passende Überschrift.*

paragraph 1 (lines 1–10)	paragraph 2 (lines 11–15)	paragraph 3 (lines 16–20)	paragraph 4 (lines 21–28)	paragraph 5 (lines 29–36)	paragraph 6 (lines 37–40)
E	C	D	G	A	B

Aufgabe 2

✎ **Hinweis:** *Im Lesetext über Bethany Hamilton fehlen vier Sätze. Diese sind im Text*
✎ *mit (1), (2), (3) und (4) gekennzeichnet. Die fehlenden Sätze (sowie einen weiteren,*
✎ *nicht passenden Satz) findest du in Aufgabe 2. Erschließe aus dem Zusammenhang,*
✎ *welcher Satz zu welcher Textstelle passt und trage den jeweiligen Buchstaben in die*
✎ *Tabelle ein.*
✎ *Hinweise im Text:*
✎ *(1) F: "I was more scared ..." (Z. 19 f.)*
✎ *(2) A: "... surfing competitions have taken her to South America, ..." (Z. 25 f.)*
✎ *(3) C: "Bethany is not only a star in the water." (Z. 29)*
✎ *(4) D: "This is what she has to say to young people: ..." (Z. 39)*

Vokabelhinweise:

to compete with: sich messen mit, gegen jmd. antreten
successful: erfolgreich
to be hopeless: ohne Hoffnung sein

(0)	(1)	(2)	(3)	(4)
B	F	**A**	C	D

Aufgabe 3

✎ **Hinweis:** *Überprüfe hier, ob die Aussagen zum Lesetext richtig oder falsch sind.*

a) True
✎   **Hinweis:** Z. 4 f.

b) False
✎   **Hinweis:** Z. 13 f.

c) False
   Hinweis: *Z. 18 f.*
d) True
   Hinweis: *Z. 39 f.*

Aufgabe 4

a)	b)	c)	d)
line(s) 6–7	line(s) 11–12	line(s) 17–18	line(s) 29–30

Aufgabe 5

a) (in) 2005
   Hinweis: *Z. 22 f.*
b) (it's) Soul Surfer
   Hinweis: *Z. 31*
c) shark attack survivors
   oder: (other) amputees (worldwide)
   Hinweis: *Z. 35 f.*

D Text Production

Allgemeiner Hinweis: *Auch in diesem Prüfungsteil darfst du ein zweisprachiges Wörterbuch verwenden. Entscheide dich bei der Bearbeitung entweder für die E-Mail oder für die Bildergeschichte.*

1. Correspondence: E-Mail

Hinweis: *Berücksichtige beim Verfassen deiner E-Mail die allgemeinen Hinweise zu Umfang und Form, die in der Aufgabenstellung beschrieben sind. Verfasse eine verständliche E-Mail in ganzen Sätzen. Bringe beim Schreiben die Vorgaben zum Inhalt ein und ergänze sie, wenn du möchtest, auch durch eigene Gedanken.*

Hi Chris,

Would you like to take part in an international football (*oder AmE:* soccer) camp with me? I went to an international football camp in London last summer and it was great! I stayed there for two weeks and I was able to improve my skills a lot. It was the first time that I got training from professional trainers and I also met some football stars! Just imagine, I even shook hands with Theo Walcott and I also got some autographs!

It was also great that I was able to meet other boys and girls from all over the world. At the weekends we went sightseeing in London. We visited the Emirates stadium, went shopping and one night we went to a fantastic disco.

I am going to apply *(bewerben)* for the football camp again this year. Do you want to join me? You can find some more information on the internet: www.soccer-campsinternational.com/arsenal-soccer-camp

I'm looking forward to hearing from you soon.

Best wishes,
Angela

2. Picture-based Writing:

Hinweis: *Sieh dir die Bilder genau an, bevor du mit dem Schreiben beginnst. Beachte auch die Aufschriften: „Happy birthday", „remote controlled shark" (ferngesteuerter Hai), „lifeguard" (Rettungsschwimmer), „Help!" und „Ron's pedal boat". Berücksichtige beim Schreiben der Bildergeschichte die allgemeinen Hinweise zu Umfang und Form, die in der Aufgabenstellung angegeben sind. Denke an Einleitung, Überleitung und Schluss und verwende in deinem Text auch die wörtliche Rede. Wie die Geschichte beginnen könnte, findest du ebenfalls auf dem Angabenblatt. Verfasse die Geschichte in der Zeitform <u>simple past</u> (Signalwort: last year).*

Shark alarm

Paul always wanted to have a remote-controlled shark. Last year, on his birthday, he finally got one as a present from his parents. He was very happy. Paul took the shark with him the next time he went to the seaside. It was a sunny and warm day and some people were out on the sea in pedal boats. "The perfect moment to try my remote-controlled shark", Paul thought. He wanted to scare the people a little by letting the shark swim around their pedal boats. It worked wonderfully! Two ladies with hats got really frightened when they saw the shark's fin *(Flosse)* going around their boat. One of them threw her arms up into the air and the other one screamed "Help!" The life guard came right away and was very angry with Paul. "Leave the beach – now! You are not allowed to come back with your shark anymore!" he shouted. Paul was disappointed that the life guard didn't see the fun of it.

Notenschlüssel

Notenstufen	1	2	3	4	5	6
Punkte	80–68	67–55	54–41	40–27	26–13	12–0

A Listening

Allgemeiner Hinweis: *Die Hörtexte werden in der Prüfung von einer CD abgespielt, und zwar insgesamt zweimal und ohne zusätzliche Erklärungen oder Unterbrechungen. Du bekommst Zeit, dir die Aufgaben anzusehen, bevor du den dazugehörigen Text das erste Mal hörst. Während des Zuhörens, bzw. im Anschluss daran, bearbeitest du dann die jeweilige Aufgabe.*

Part 1

1   WAITER: Yours was the white wine, wasn't it, madam?
    MOTHER: Um, no, that was for my husband. The red is for me.
    WAITER: I'm sorry, here you are madam.
    MOTHER: Thanks.
5   WAITER: And the white for you, sir.
    FATHER: Thank you.
    WAITER: Roast beef with chips and mixed vegetables. Is this for you, sir?
    FATHER: Er, no. It's for my daughter. I ordered the fish.
    WAITER: Ah, the fish. The fish with rice and broccoli.
10 FATHER: Right.
    WAITER: Here you are, young lady. Your roast beef. Enjoy your meal.
    RACHEL: Thank you.
    MOTHER: Hmm … that looks fantastic. I should have taken that, too, but I'm sure
        my fish soup will be fine.
15 WAITER: Okay, fish with rice and broccoli. Here you are, sir. And the soup for you,
        madam. Hope you enjoy it.
    FATHER & MOTHER: Thank you.

	mother	father	daughter
white wine		✓	
red wine	✓		
fish		✓	
fish soup	✓		
rice		✓	

	mother	father	daughter
broccoli		✓	
beef steak			
roast beef			✓
chips			✓
vegetables			✓
vegetable soup			
	1 point	1 point	1 point

Hinweis: *In der Auswahlliste findest du zwei Gerichte („beef steak" und „vegetable soup"), die im Hörtext nicht vorkommen.*

Part 2

1 SPEAKER: ... and in our restaurant we have a wide selection of meals today.
   Come to our Sandwich Corner and create your own sandwich! Choose from a variety of bread and a range of meats and cheeses. Every sandwich costs just £2.50.
5 Today's special offer in the Sandwich Corner and only available between four and five this afternoon: buy one and get one free!
   At our Salad Bar, you can make your own salad for only £3.99. Pay just £1 more, and you can choose from a selection of cold ham, sausages, eggs and fish to go with your salad.
10 If you prefer a warm meal, Italian food is our speciality this week. We offer some of the most popular Italian dishes. Prices start at £4.50. For children we have halfprice meals for only £2.25.
   These delicious offers are all available now in our restaurant. Come and join us on the fifth floor.

Vokabelhinweise:
Z. 1: selection: Auswahl
Z. 5: available: erhältlich
Z. 10: to prefer: etw. vorziehen
Z. 14: floor: Etage, Stockwerk

1. From **4** to **5** o'clock you get two sandwiches and pay for only one.
2. Creating your own salad costs £ **3.99**.
3. Pay only £ **1** more and you can add ham or eggs to your salad.
4. The cheapest warm meal is £ **4.50**.
5. Children can have an Italian dish for £ **2.25**.
6. The restaurant is on the **5(th)** floor.

Part 3

1 ANNE: Mmm, this soup tastes delicious. Did you make it yourself?
   BETTY: Yes, but it's nothing special, just my usual cream of vegetable soup.
   ANNE: But it really is fantastic. What did you put in it?
   BETTY: Well, some chopped cabbage, a bit of celery, carrots, and some fried onions.
5   And then I added spices, of course, and salt and pepper and so on …
   ANNE: Hmm, but this has got potatoes and tomatoes in it, hasn't it?
   BETTY: Yes, potatoes, I always use them. And I normally use tomatoes too, but I
      didn't have any today.
   ANNE: And the green bits? What are they? Beans?
10 BETTY: No, no, they're peas.
   ANNE: Hmm, and there's no meat in it?
   BETTY: No, there is. I put a bit of bacon in it. Is that okay for you?
   ANNE: Yeah, of course. It gives it a really lovely flavour.
   BETTY: Yes. I think so, too.
15 ANNE: Are all the vegetables from your garden?
   BETTY: Yes, everything. Only one thing isn't: the mushrooms.
   ANNE: Well, it really is delicious.
   BETTY: Thank you. Would you like some more?

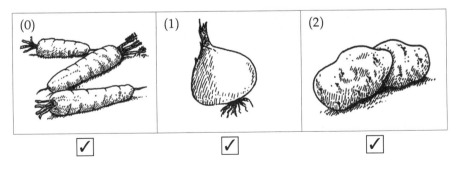

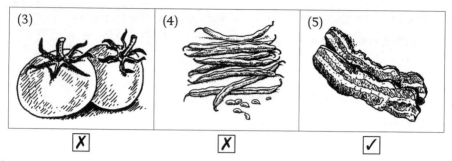

(3)	(4)	(5)
✗	✗	✓

✎ **Hinweis:** *Kreuze hier unbedingt <u>sowohl</u> die Zutaten an, die in der Gemüsesuppe ent-*
✎ *halten (✓), <u>als auch</u> solche, die <u>nicht</u> (✗) enthalten sind. Es darf kein Kästchen leer*
✎ *bleiben!*

Part 4

1 PAMELA: Hello.

   MIKE: Hi, Pamela. It's me, Mike.

   PAMELA: Hi, Mike, nice to hear from you again. Are you back?

   MIKE: Yes, I've been back since Monday. I thought it would be nice to meet up for

5   a meal again. How about Friday evening?

   PAMELA: Well, that's a nice idea, Mike, but I'm afraid I'm rather busy right now.

     On Friday I probably won't be home until 9 or something …

   MIKE: Oh, I see. Well, what about Saturday, then?

   PAMELA: That sounds fine. Where would you like to go?

10 MIKE: Well, what do you think about an Indian restaurant? Shall we try one?

   PAMELA: I'm sorry, but Indian food is far too hot for me.

   MIKE: Okay. Why don't we go to the Red Lion, then? They do good food, and

     they have a lot of vegetarian meals. Have you been there? Do you know the pub?

   PAMELA: Yes, I know it well. Everybody goes there for their fresh vegetables and

15 baked potatoes. Let's go there. How about 7 o'clock?

   MIKE: I think it opens at 7, so I'll pick you up at your house at half past six. Okay?

   PAMELA: Fine. See you on Saturday then.

   MIKE: Thanks. Bye now.

   PAMELA: Bye, Mike.

	T	F
1. He wants to go out on Friday.	✓	
2. Pamela wants to stay at home till 9.		✓
3. She likes hot Indian meals.		✓

		T	F
4.	The Red Lion pub is popular because of its baked potatoes.	☑	☐
5.	The pub is closed till 7.	☑	☐
6.	Mike wants to pick Pamela up at 7.30.	☐	☑

B Use of English

Hinweis: *In diesem Teil werden deine Grammatik- und Wortschatzkenntnisse sowie deine Kenntnisse der Redemittel geprüft. Beachte auch die Rechtschreibung, vor allem dann, wenn die Wörter wie in Aufgabe 3 schon vorgegeben sind.*

Aufgabe 1

Hinweis: *Die Abfolge der Bilder und Sätze stimmt nicht überein. Lies zunächst die Sätze durch, suche dann das Bild, das vom Sinn her passen könnte und schreibe schließlich das entsprechende Wort dafür in die Lücke. Bild 4 („chicken" oder „turkey") wird nicht gebraucht.*

Tom is having a ~~party~~. A lot of guests/people/friends are coming. Everything is ready. The ~~plates~~ are on the table. The fridge/refrigerator/freezer is full of food and there is enough pizza for everybody. But one thing is missing – the chocolate cake Tom's sister wanted to make for him.

Aufgabe 2

Hinweis: *Bei dieser Übung ist es hilfreich, nach Signalwörtern zu suchen, die dir einen Hinweis auf die richtige Zeitform geben:*

Signalwörter:		Zeitform:
fifty years ago	→	*simple past*
since	→	*present perfect*
today	→	*simple present*

Falls du dir bei dieser Aufgabe unsicher warst, kannst du in der Kurzgrammatik im Band „Training Quali" auf S. 90 ff. nachschlagen. Verwende im 2. Satz nach „if" („wenn/falls") auch das „simple past", da sich alles in der Vergangenheit abspielt.

Food from other countries <u>has become</u> very popular in Britain. Fifty years ago most people <u>went</u> to a pub if they <u>didn't want</u> to eat at home. Since the 1980s a lot of foreign restaurants <u>have opened</u> all over Britain. Today, there <u>are</u> Chinese restaurants everywhere.

Aufgabe 3

Hinweis: *Hier musst du die Wörter in die richtige Reihenfolge bringen und jeweils einen sinnvollen Satz bilden. Manchmal gibt es verschiedene Möglichkeiten.*

1. Have you ever been to the restaurant near the station?

2. Yes, I have already been there three times this month. / Yes, I have been there three times this month already. / Yes, I have been there already three times this month.

3. What is the food there like? / What is the food like there?

4. The food is great/cheap but not cheap/great. / The food is not great/cheap but cheap/great.

Aufgabe 4

Hinweis: *Kreise das Wort ein, das grammatikalisch oder sinngemäß passt. Nur <u>ein</u> Wort pro Auswahlreihe ist richtig.*
Vokabelhinweise zu den richtigen Lösungen:
usually: normalerweise, gewöhnlich
there: dort
which: leitet hier einen Relativsatz ein (... eine Mahlzeit, <u>die</u> ...); „who" wird nur bei Personen verwendet; „what" ist ein Fragewort (was?); „whose" bezeichnet den Genitiv (dessen/wessen)
with other pupils: mit anderen Schülern
to enjoy themselves: sich amüsieren, hier im Sinn von: „eine gute Zeit haben"

British pupils (0) • **almost** • **nearly** • **suddenly** • usually • have lunch in their school cafeteria. (1) • *That* • *Their* • There • *Where* • they can get drinks, snacks or even a meal (2) • *what* • which • *who* • *whose* • is quite cheap. They sit together with (3) • *a* • *another* • other • *our* • pupils from their class, have a chat and enjoy (4) • *each other* • *them* • themselves • *they* • before they go to their afternoon lessons.

Aufgabe 5

Hinweis: *Lies dir zunächst Toms Antworten durch. Notiere dann eine passende Frage. Meist gibt es mehrere richtige Möglichkeiten.*

Peter: Hi, Tom. How are you?

Tom: I'm fine. I'm on a trip through Germany.

Peter: Oh. Where are you?

Tom In Munich. I'm staying in a hostel.

Peter: OK. How much does it cost? / How much is it per night? / ...?

Tom: € 28 per night, which is not bad.

Peter: Great. What's the weather like? / How is the weather? / What about the weather? / ...

Tom: It's sunny and warm.

Peter: Lovely. When will you be back (home)? / When are you coming back /home? / ...?

Tom: I'll be back next weekend.

Peter: Great. See you then. Have fun.

Tom: Thanks. Bye.

C Reading Comprehension

Allgemeiner Hinweis: *Lies den Text zunächst einmal durch, damit du weißt, wovon er handelt. Schlage nur diejenigen unbekannten Wörter nach, die zum Verständnis des Textes unbedingt nötig sind. Nimm dir Zeit beim Durchsehen der Aufgaben, damit du verstehst, welche Lösung gesucht ist. Hier lohnt es sich, das ein oder andere Wort nachzuschlagen. Konzentriere dich nun auf die Stellen im Text, die zur Beantwortung der jeweiligen Aufgabe von Bedeutung sind.*

Vokabelhinweise:

Z. 2 f.: inhabitant: Einwohner

Z. 3: port: Hafen

Z. 5: to invent: erfinden

Z. 6: Earl: Graf

Z. 7: to command the Navy: die Kriegsflotte/Marine kommandieren

Z. 11: slice: Scheibe

Z. 13: convenient: praktisch, bequem

Z. 18: cucumber: Gurke

Z. 24: competition: Wettbewerb

Z. 26: groceries: Lebensmittel

Z. 31: weight: Gewicht

Aufgabe 1

Hinweis: *Notiere die passende Überschrift zum jeweiligen Abschnitt des Lesetextes. Schreibe auch auf, welche Überschrift übrig bleibt („extra title").*

paragraph 1 (lines 1–4)	paragraph 2 (lines 5–14)	paragraph 3 (lines 15–20)	paragraph 4 (lines 21–29)	paragraph 5 (lines 30–36)	The extra title is
D	F	A	E	B	C

Aufgabe 2

Hinweis: *Kreuze an, ob die Aussage richtig (true: T), falsch (false: F) oder nicht im Text (not in the text: N) ist.*

	T	F	N
1. The distance between Sandwich and London is 18 miles. **Hinweis:** *Z. 1 f.*		✓	
2. John Montagu often won when he played cards.			✓
3. Working men prefer cucumber sandwiches. **Hinweis:** *Z. 18 f.*		✓	
4. Max King took part in a sandwich-making competition.			✓
5. A study shows that eating fast food can make you overweight. **Hinweis:** *Z. 30 f.*	✓		
6. Mr Brightman, the owner of a sandwich restaurant, is married. **Hinweis:** *Z. 32 f.*	✓		

Aufgabe 3

Hinweis: *Antworte in kurzen Sätzen oder Stichpunkten. Schreibe keine vollständigen Sätze aus dem Text ab.*

1. 5,000 / 5000
   Hinweis: *Z. 2*
2. he commanded the British Navy
   Hinweis: *Z. 7*
3. playing cards / (he loved to) play cards
   Hinweis: *Z. 8*

4. (because) he wanted to hold his cards and eat at the same time / (because) he wanted to play (cards) and eat at the same time / (because) he wanted to eat without (a) knife and (a) fork
   / Hinweis: *Z. 9 ff.*

5. (because) they saw how convenient it was / (they saw) it was convenient
   / Hinweis: *Z. 12 f.*

6. (a) butty
   / Hinweis: *Z. 19*

7. (because) the smell gets into the bread/into it
   / Hinweis: *Z. 26 f.*

8. freshly-baked bread / (filling of) organic vegetables / meat straight out of the oven
   / Hinweis: *Z. 34 ff. (delicious: lecker, köstlich)*

D Text Production

/ **Allgemeiner Hinweis:** *Schreibe entweder die E-Mail oder die Bildergeschichte. Du*
/ *darfst ein zweisprachiges Wörterbuch verwenden. Die Lösungsbeispiele sind bewusst*
/ *etwas länger gehalten als in den Angaben vorgegeben. So bekommst du verschiede-*
/ *ne Ideen für deine eigene Lösung.*

1. Correspondence: E-Mail

/ **Hinweis:** *Berücksichtige beim Schreiben deiner E-Mail die Vorgaben zu Umfang,*
/ *Form und Inhalt, wie sie in der Aufgabenstellung aufgeführt sind. Da du die E-Mail*
/ *an deine Gasteltern sendest, sollte sie persönlichen Charakter haben. Schreibe in gan-*
/ *zen Sätzen und achte darauf, dass deine E-Mail in sich schlüssig und verständlich*
/ *ist. Der folgende Wortschatz kann dir beim Verfassen der E-Mail nützlich sein:*
/ *– Anrede: Dear ... / Hello, ...*
/ *– sich für die Zeit in der Gastfamilie bedanken: Thanks that I could ...*
/ *– Gefallen ausdrücken: It was great that ... / I liked ... / It was very nice that ...*
/ *– Unterkunft: accommodation, room, house, garden, balcony etc.*
/ *– Essen: breakfast, lunch, dinner*
/ *– Haustiere: pets (e.g. dog, cat, budgie, guinea pig), to pet, to feed, to go for a walk,*
/ *well-bred (gut erzogen), cute (niedlich)*
/ *– Aktivitäten: sports (e.g. swimming, cycling, jogging, playing football), go to the*
/ *cinema, play an instrument etc.*
/ *– Fotos im Anhang: to attach some photos*

Dear Sarah and Paul,

How are you? I hope everybody is fine.
Thanks again that I could stay with you! You made me feel so comfortable. I liked my room very much. I also loved to sit on the balcony and look at all the pretty flowers in your garden. And of course I miss Kitty, your cute little cat that came over to visit me every morning. It was also so much fun to go to the pub, the cinema or the Art Festival in the evening. I have attached some photos – and I hope you like them, too.
My trip back home was okay. The plane was on time so that I arrived in the early afternoon. My family picked me up at the airport. My parents are happy that I'm back home again and my mother is very pleased about the earrings that I bought for her at the festival. But my brother doesn't like the T-Shirt I gave him as a present. He doesn't know much about fashion ... ☺!
I hope that you'll be able to see my family and me when you come to Germany next year. You're always welcome and I'm really looking forward to meeting you again.
Hope to hear from you soon.

Take care!

Yours, Isabel

2. Picture-based Writing:

Hinweis: Berücksichtige beim Schreiben der Bildergeschichte die Vorgaben zu Umfang und Form, die in der Aufgabenstellung angegeben sind. Schreibe die Geschichte in der Zeitform „simple past" (One afternoon, Emily called Chris ...), zum Teil musst du die Verlaufsform („past progressive form") verwenden. Betrachte alle Bilder genau, damit du keine wichtigen Details übersiehst (z. B. in Bild 4: Uhr; unbemerktes Hereinschleichen der Katzen ins Esszimmer). Auch der Text und die Symbole in den Sprechblasen enthalten wichtige Informationen.
Denke beim Schreiben an die Einleitung und den Schluss-Satz sowie an die Verwen-

dung der wörtlichen Rede. Schreibe in ganzen Sätzen, baue den Handlungsverlauf
logisch auf und achte darauf, dass die Geschichte auch sprachlich gut verständlich
ist.

Der folgende Wortschatz kann dir beim Verfassen der Geschichte nützlich sein:
- *Bild 1: verliebt sein in:* be in love with, *einladen:* to invite, *Einladung:* invitation, *die Katzen schliefen in ihren Körbchen:* the cats *were sleeping* in their baskets
- *Bild 2: kochen:* to cook, *Schüssel:* bowl, *Herd:* stove, *Ofen:* oven, *sich interessieren für:* to be interested in, *beobachten:* to watch
- *Bild 3: den Bus verpassen:* to miss the bus, *den Tisch decken:* to lay the table/to set the table, *anrufen:* to call/to phone
- *Bild 4: sich beeilen:* to hurry, *hereinschleichen:* to sneak in, to crawl inside
- *Bild 5: Unordnung:* mess

Dinner for two

One afternoon, Emily called Chris to invite him for dinner. She asked him to come the following day at 8 pm. Chris was in love with Emily and was happy about the invitation. While Emily was talking to Chris, her two cats, Jerry and Johnny were sleeping in their baskets.

The next day, Emily was in her kitchen preparing the meal. She had a big fish in the oven, a pot with potatoes on the stove and a large bowl full of salad on the kitchen counter. Her two cats were watching her the whole time.

Just before 8 pm, Chris called Emily. He sounded disappointed. "I'm sorry, but I missed the bus!" he told her. Emily was already putting all the nice food on the table, but she said: "No worries, I'll pick you up, Chris." Emily left the dining room in a hurry, so she did not see that Johnny and Jerry had crawled inside before she closed the door. They were very hungry.

At 8 pm it was dinner time. Jerry and Johnny were sharing the fish on the table. They just loved it! For poor Emily and Chris they only left the potatoes and the salad, which were lying on the floor.

Notenschlüssel

Notenstufen	1	2	3	4	5	6
Punkte	80–71	70–60	59–46	45–32	31–18	17–0

A Listening

Allgemeiner Hinweis: Der Hörverstehenstest besteht aus drei Teilen. In dem Test geht es um ein Paar, das in den USA Urlaub macht. Zu jedem Text, den du von der CD hörst, gibt es eine Aufgabe („Task"), die du mithilfe der Informationen aus dem jeweiligen Hörtext bearbeiten sollst.
Verschaffe dir zuerst einen Überblick über die Aufgaben. Du hörst die Texte je zwei Mal. Du kannst die Aufgaben entweder während des Zuhörens und/oder im Anschluss daran bearbeiten.

Part 1

1 MIKE/KATE: Hello. Hi.
RECEPTIONIST: Hello there. Can I help you?
MIKE: Yes, we've reserved a room ... um ... on the internet.
RECEPTIONIST: OK. Could I have your passports, please?
5 KATE: Sure.
RECEPTIONIST: Is this your first stay here?
MIKE: Well, not in the US, but it's our first visit to Washington.
RECEPTIONIST: OK. Great. Three nights, right. Leaving on Friday.
KATE: Yeah. That's right.
10 RECEPTIONIST: Could I have your credit card, please?
MIKE: Sure.
KATE: Um ... we wanted to know if you had a room at the back, you know, away
      from the road.
RECEPTIONIST: Well, actually, you're in room 430, which *is* at the back.
15 MIKE: Great. Thanks. And all the rooms have Wi-Fi, don't they?
RECEPTIONIST: Yes, they do. You'll need the password, it's JFK 430.
KATE: Great. Thanks. Um ... we're booked on a tour of the White House tomor-
      row morning.
MIKE: Yeah, is it far from here?
20 RECEPTIONIST: Actually it is. But you can take a taxi or a bus. There's a bus stop
      right outside the hotel.
MIKE: OK. What about breakfast?
RECEPTIONIST: Breakfast is served from 6.30 till 10. The breakfast room's in the
      basement. The elevator is behind the bar, on your right.
25 KATE: OK, thanks.
RECEPTIONIST: Enjoy your stay.

1. The receptionist wants to see their **passport(s)/(credit card)**.
   Hinweis: Z. 4/Z. 10

2. It's Kate and Mike's **first/1st** visit to Washington DC.
   Hinweis: Z. 7

3. They are leaving on **Friday**.
   Hinweis: Z. 8

4. They would like a room which is at **the back** of the hotel.
   Hinweis: Z. 12

5. The Wi-Fi password is **JFK 430**.
   Hinweis: Z. 16; *konzentriere dich hier besonders, um die Buchstaben-Zahlen-Kombination richtig zu verstehen.*

6. They should take a **taxi** or a bus to get to the White House.
   Hinweis: Z. 20

7. The bus stop is **(right) outside** the hotel.
   Hinweis: Z. 20

8. Breakfast is from **6.30** till **10**.
   Hinweis: Z. 23

Part 2

1 GUIDE: Welcome to the White House. Our tour begins with some history. It took eight years to build the White House, from 1792 to 1800. Today the White House is where the president and his family live but it is also where he and his staff, over 1,500 people, work. It has 132 rooms on 6 floors. Here are some
5 more figures about the White House. *(Fade begins)* There are …

GUIDE: You're now standing in the Map Room. On the walls you can see different maps of Washington DC and the world. Today meetings, television interviews, small teas or even classical concerts are held here. *(Fade begins)* It was …

10 GUIDE: If you look out of the window you'll see a tennis court. Soon after Barack Obama became president, it was changed so that people could play basketball on it as well. President Obama is a big basketball fan. He does not play alone, though. He often invites school teams, college teams and also professionals to play at the White House. *(Fade begins)* It is …

15 GUIDE: Also outside you'll see one of the White House's latest projects: the First Lady's garden. Here Mrs Obama is growing vegetables so that her family – but also guests – get fresh vegetables. Mrs Obama hopes the garden will be a learn-

ing experience where visitors to the White House can see how fresh food can be part of a healthy diet. *(Fade begins)* If you ...

20 GUIDE: This is the White House Library. The room was not always full of books and paintings. Many years ago it was a laundry room, where the first families' clothes were washed, dried and ironed. *(Fade begins)* If you ...

GUIDE: You are now in the Family Theater. This is a movie theater with 42 seats where the First Family and their guests can watch movies, sports games and
25 TV shows. *(Fade begins)* In March ...

✔ **Allgemeiner Hinweis:** *Folgende Fragewörter solltest du verstehen, um die Fragen*
✔ *richtig beantworten zu können:*
✔ *how many? – wie viele?*
✔ *where? – wo?*
✔ *who? – wer?*
✔ *what? – was?*

1. 132
✔ Hinweis: *Z. 4*

2. (on the) wall(s)
✔ Hinweis: *Z. 6*

3. school teams/college teams/professionals
✔ Hinweis: *Z. 13*

4. (the) garden (project)
✔ Hinweis: *Z. 17 f.*

5. paintings
✔ Hinweis: *Z. 21 (except = außer)*

6. (in the) Family Theater/movie theater/Theater
✔ Hinweis: *Z. 23*

Part 3

1 MIKE: You know my idea about hiking through the Grand Canyon in one day?
   KATE: Yeah.
   MIKE: Well, we can forget that. It takes 12 hours to go down one side and up the
       other. And it's really hot down there at this time of the year. Over 35° in some
5   places.
   KATE: Can't we camp for one night?
   MIKE: Camp? No, we'd need a special permit to do that. And it's too late to get
       one now anyway.
   KATE: Oh. OK.
10 MIKE: I've got another idea, though. We could go on a helicopter tour. There's one
       here. You fly through the Grand Canyon, land somewhere, have a picnic and
       then fly back. Three hours in total.
   KATE: But what does it cost?
   MIKE: Hold on. Oh. Mmm. Ah, 499 dollars per person.
15 KATE: Well, that's expensive for 3 hours.
   MIKE: Here's another tour. Wait a second. OK, this one goes from Grand Canyon
       Airport and lasts about 30 minutes. But you don't land anywhere.
   KATE: Is that cheaper?
   MIKE: Hold on. It says … 199 dollars … no, wait … 154 dollars if you book on-
20   line.
   KATE: Sounds cool, doesn't it?
   MIKE: Shall I book?
   KATE: Yeah.
   MIKE: When are we at the Grand Canyon?
25 KATE: On Monday.
   MIKE: OK. How about booking for Tuesday at … er 10.30?
   KATE: Sounds perfect.
   MIKE: Great.

	Hiking tour	**Helicopter tour**	**Tour from Grand Canyon Airport**
Costs per person?	No costs	$ 499 (Z. 14)	$ 154 online booking (Z. 19 f.)
Hours/minutes?	12 hours (Z. 3)	3 hours	30 minutes (Z. 16 f.)
Problems?	(really) hot/35° (Z. 4 f.)/ (need a) permit (Z. 7) (for camping)	(too) expensive (Z. 15)	no stop in the Canyon

E 2014-4

B Use of English

Allgemeiner Hinweis: *In diesem Prüfungsteil musst du dein Wissen im Bereich Wortschatz, Grammatik und Rechtschreibung unter Beweis stellen. Auch musst du eine Sprechsituation bewältigen, wie sie im Alltag vorkommen kann.*

Aufgabe 1

Hinweis: *In dieser Aufgabe werden deine Wortschatz- und Grammatikkenntnisse geprüft. Du findest bereits eine Auswahl an Wörtern im Kasten. Wähle die passenden aus. Im Folgenden findest du Hinweise zu den richtigen Lösungen:*

1 *who: leitet hier einen Relativsatz ein („... die bereits einen Studienplatz an einem College hat."); „which" ist hier nicht möglich, da es sich bei Julia um eine Person handelt. Siehe auch S. 87 f. in der Kurzgrammatik.*
2 *She ... enjoys work<u>ing</u> on the computer: sie arbeitet gerne am Computer (enjoy + Verb mit -ing-Form).*
3 *to be good at: gut sein in*
4 *got: simple past von „get" (bekommen)*
5 *would like: würde gerne*
6 *to apply for: sich bewerben für/um*

Julia, 17, is one of (0) <u>of</u> the students at her high school (1) <u>who</u> has already got a place at college. She really enjoys (2) <u>working</u> on the computer and she's very good (3) <u>at</u> designing websites. On her last birthday she (4) <u>got</u> a new computer from her parents. In her vacation Julia (5) <u>would</u> like to do work experience at a software firm in Boston. She has already applied (6) <u>for</u> a job at three different companies but she's still waiting to hear from them.

Aufgabe 2

Hinweis: *Hier geht es nur um den Wortschatz. Ergänze den Lückentext mit den passenden Substantiven (Namenwörtern). Versuche, die fehlenden Wörter aus dem Textzusammenhang zu erschließen. Auch sind als Hilfestellung die Anfangsbuchstaben der gesuchten Wörter angegeben*

1 *satchel: Schultasche; schedule: hier: Stundenplan*
2 *dictionary: hier: Wörterbuch*
3 *subject: Schulfach*
4 *gym/gymnasium: Turnhalle*

Tom is a (0) <u>student</u> at a high school in Boston. Every morning he checks his (1) <u>school bag/satchel/schedule</u> to see if he has everything he needs: his books, his calculator and his pencil case. As he is doing a Spanish test today, Tom has to take his (2) <u>dictionary</u> to look up the words he doesn't know. He likes biology and English very much, but his favorite (3) <u>subject</u> is sports. In summer students use the sports fields but in winter they do sport in the (4) <u>gym/gymnasium</u>.

Aufgabe 3

Hinweis: *Hier werden deine Grammatikkenntnisse geprüft. Setze die vorgegebenen Verben in die richtige Zeitform. Beachte die Signalwörter, um die richtige Zeitform zu erkennen.*

Signalwort	Zeit	Besonderheit
1 *two weeks ago*	*simple past*	*„began" = unregelmäßiges Verb*
2 *two weeks ago*	*simple past*	*I, he, she, it wasn't*
3 *„isn't having" zeigt an, dass die Zeitebene nun wieder die Gegenwart ist*	*simple present*	*Während „isn't having" die Verlaufsform der Gegenwart darstellt, muss in die Lücke die Form des simple present („is").*
4 *every Saturday*	*simple present*	*he, she, it works*
5 *for over a year now*	*present perfect*	*he, she, it has*
6 *if/next year (if-Satz Typ I)*	*will-future*	*Statt „will (buy)" ist im if-Satz auch die Verwendung von „can (buy)" möglich.*

As everybody (0) <u>knows</u>, driving a car is very important in the USA. In some states people can get a driving license when they are 16. About two weeks ago Steven (1) <u>began</u> learning how to drive. The first lesson (2) <u>wasn't</u> easy. He isn't having lessons at a driving school because his father (3) <u>is</u> his instructor. Every Saturday Steven (4) <u>works</u> at a local supermarket. He (5) <u>has had</u> the job for over a year now. If he saves enough money, he (6) <u>will buy/can buy</u> himself a decent second-hand car next year.

Aufgabe 4

Hinweis: *Bei dieser Aufgabe geht es darum, dass du dich in Alltagssituationen angemessen ausdrücken kannst. Lies dir zunächst die Antwortsätze durch, damit du weißt, <u>wonach</u> du fragen sollst. Manchmal kannst du das Verb (z. B. ask, start) des Antwortsatzes auch für deine Frage verwenden. Beachte bei deinen Fragen die Umschreibung mit „to do": (evtl. Fragewort) + do (can, may …) + you + Verb …?*

Tim:	Can you help me, please? I have to give a talk about American schools.
Jill:	Of course, I can help you.
Tim:	<u>May I</u>/<u>Can I</u>/<u>Could I ask you</u> some questions?
Jill:	Sure. Just feel free to ask.
Tim:	<u>When do you start (school)</u>/<u>When does school start</u> in the morning?
Jill:	We start at 9. But before that I meet my friends.
Tim:	<u>Where do you meet</u> them?
Jill:	In the school cafeteria. We have breakfast there.
Tim:	<u>Do you bring</u>/<u>eat</u>/<u>take</u>/<u>have</u> your own food?
Jill:	No we don't. We have to buy the food at the cafeteria.

C Reading Comprehension

Allgemeiner Hinweis: *Im Lesetext geht es um die beiden Töchter des amerikanischen Präsidenten Barack Obama.*

Nach dem ersten Lesen solltest du den Inhalt des Textes im Wesentlichen verstanden haben. Schlage nur diejenigen Wörter nach, die du unbedingt zum Verständnis benötigst. Bei der Bearbeitung der Aufgaben ist es nötig, dass du zunächst diejenigen Textstellen findest, auf die sich die Aufgaben beziehen, und diese nochmals konzentriert durchliest, ehe du die Lösungen aufschreibst.

Vokabelhinweise:

Z. 1: in the public eye: im Auge der Öffentlichkeit, von vielen Menschen beobachtet

Z. 9: incredible: unglaublich

Z. 20: to yawn: gähnen

Z. 21 f.: to remind: erinnern an

Z. 23: environment: hier: Umgebung, Umfeld

Z. 25: staff: Belegschaft, Mitarbeiter

Z. 29: responsibility: Verantwortung

Z. 32: college: Hochschule

Z. 37: to be proud of sb./sth.: stolz sein auf jmd./etw.

Z. 40 f.: to have a sleepover: bei jemanden übernachten

Z. 44: to deserve sth.: etw. verdienen

Kasten: rule: Regel

Aufgabe 1

Hinweis: *Wenn du die Überschriften richtig zuordnest, zeigt dies, dass du den Inhalt des Textes im Wesentlichen verstanden hast.*

Vokabel: chores = Hausarbeit

paragraph 1 (lines 1–4)	C
paragraph 2 (lines 5–10)	G
paragraph 3 (lines 11–20)	A
paragraph 4 (lines 21–32)	B
paragraph 5 (lines 33–38)	E
paragraph 6 (lines 39–44)	F

Aufgabe 2

Hinweis: *Für jede Lücke ergibt nur jeweils ein Auswahl-Satz im Textzusammenhang einen Sinn. Beachte, dass ein Satz in keine Lücke passt.*

(0)	(1)	(2)	(3)	(4)	(5)
C	**G**	**D**	**F**	**B**	**A**

Aufgabe 3

Hinweis: *Beantworte die Fragen in Stichpunkten, indem du die Schlüsselwörter dem Lesetext entnimmst.*

1. Air Force One

   Hinweis: *Z. 5 f; gefragt wird nach dem Namen des Flugzeugs des US-Präsidenten ("<u>What is</u> the President's aircraft <u>called</u>?").*

2. (on/at the) weekend

   Hinweis: *siehe Kasten, Absatz „Technology"; gefragt wird, wann die Töchter das Internet nutzen dürfen („allowed to use").*

3. make (their own) beds/set the table/take (the) dogs for a walk

   Hinweis: *Z. 26 ff.*

4. (have) sleepovers/(go to the) shopping (mall)/(go to the) movies

   Hinweis: *Z. 40 f.*

Aufgabe 4

Hinweis: *Suche nach der Stelle im Lesetext, die in der jeweiligen Frage umschrieben wird und notiere dann den (Teil)Satz als Lösung.*

1. They have met lots of well-known people …
   Hinweis: *Z. 6 f. (celebrities: Stars, Berühmtheiten)*

2. … they have to listen and smile.
   Hinweis: *Z. 18 f. (in public: in der Öffentlichkeit, vor anderen Leuten)*

3. … they're not going to be in the White House for ever./
   Not long from now they'll be at college by themselves.
   Hinweis: *Z. 30 ff. (present: gegenwärtig, momentan)*

4. … they have to write reports about what they saw …
   Hinweis: *Kasten, Absatz „Trips"*

5. … he is extremely proud of his children./They're smart …/
   … they're respectful./I could not have asked for better kids.
   Hinweis: *Z. 37 f. (opinion: Meinung)*

6. I've got tough guys with guns looking after my daughters.
   Hinweis: *Z. 43 f. (well protected: gut behütet)*

D Text Production

Allgemeiner Hinweis: *Entscheide dich <u>entweder</u> für die E-Mail <u>oder</u> für die Bildergeschichte. Du darfst ein zweisprachiges Wörterbuch verwenden. Beachte die Vorgaben zu Umfang, Form und Inhalt, die in der Aufgabenstellung beschrieben sind. Die Lösungseispiele sind jedoch bewusst etwas länger gehalten, so dass du verschiedene Ideen für deine eigene Lösung bekommst.*

1. Correspondence: E-Mail

Hinweis: *Lies dir die vorgegebene E-Mail gut durch. Du findest hier Fragen und Aufforderungen, auf die du in deiner Antwortmail eingehen sollst – du kannst aber auch eigene Ideen einbringen. Die Mail enthält viele Vokabeln und Ausdrücke, die du auch in deiner Antwort verwenden kannst. Da du das Job-Angebot annehmen möchtest, sollte deine Mail in einem höflichen und interessierten Ton geschrieben sein. Sie sollte neben dem Hauptteil auch eine Anrede (Dear/Hello Susan …), einen Schlusssatz (Looking forward to hearing from you, See you in San Francisco …), deinen Gruß (Best wishes, Take care …) und deinen Namen enthalten. Der Inhalt sollte klar verständlich sein. Dabei spielen neben Ausdruck und Grammatik auch die Rechtschreibung und eine saubere äußere Form eine Rolle.*

Hello Susan,

Thanks for your e-mail! It was fantastic to hear from you because I was actually looking for a summer job when I got your mail. I would be happy to come to San Francisco and look after Justin!

My holidays are from August 1st until mid-September and I could stay with you the whole time. I hope that's OK with you.

I have to admit that I don't have much experience of working with children. I only have two older sisters and Aunt Emma's sons are also older than me. But one of my hobbies is playing soccer and I could teach Justin to play! Does Justin play soccer?

Do you live in a house with a garden, or in a flat?

I think that my English is quite good. I've been learning it at school for four years. Every time I visit aunt Emma, I speak English with her, too.

How much free time I will have during my stay? Do you think that I could do a surfing course?

I'm really looking forward to hearing from you!

Best wishes,
(your name)

2. Creative Writing: Picture-based Story

Hinweis: Sieh dir zunächst die einzelnen Bilder genau an und versuche die Geschichte im Ganzen zu verstehen. Finde dabei die Pointe heraus (der Tintenfisch hat die Brille des Großvaters auf). Auch die Überschrift ("The big catch" – „Der große Fang") hilft dir beim Verständnis der Geschichte.

Die Überschrift sowie der Einleitungssatz für den ersten Teil (Last summer ...) und den zweiten Teil (The next day ...) sind bereits vorgegeben. Du kannst diese in deine Geschichte übernehmen. Denke daran, deinen Text durch Absätze zu gliedern. Runde deine Geschichte mit einem geeigneten Schluss ab.

Deine Geschichte sollte auch für jemanden verständlich sein, der die zugehörigen Bilder nicht kennt. Du darfst also keine wichtigen Informationen auslassen. Achte außerdem auf Wortschatz, Grammatik und Rechtschreibung. Wörtliche Rede macht deine Geschichte lebendig!

The big catch

Last summer, Steve and his granddad were at the seaside. One sunny day, when they went fishing in a small boat, a stupid thing happened to Steve's grandpa. "There's a fish on my rod!" Steve's grandpa shouted excitedly, but while he was leaning over the boat to pull the fish out of the water, his glasses fell into the sea and were gone. Grandpa was very sad.

The next day Steve went fishing again, but this time he was on his own, so he just went fishing off a jetty. All of a sudden some other anglers yelled, "An octopus!" Steve felt there was something really heavy at the other end of his rod. It was a big octopus! Steve pulled it out onto the jetty. The craziest thing was that the octopus was wearing glasses, and that they were definitely grandpa's glasses! "What a big catch!" Steve thought when he carried the octopus and the glasses back home to his grandpa.

Steve's grandpa was very surprised to see Steve's catch. "Nobody will believe this story," he murmured with relief.

Notenschlüssel

Notenstufen	1	2	3	4	5	6
Punkte	80–68	67–55	54–41	40–27	26–13	12–0

A Listening

Allgemeiner Hinweis: Der Hörverstehenstest besteht aus vier Teilen. Zu jedem Text, den du von der CD hörst, gibt es eine Aufgabe („Task"), die du mithilfe der Informationen aus dem jeweiligen Hörtext bearbeiten sollst.

Verschaffe dir zuerst einen Überblick über die Aufgaben. Du hörst die Texte je zwei Mal ohne Unterbrechungen und Erläuterungen. Die Aufgaben kannst du entweder während des Zuhörens und/oder im Anschluss daran bearbeiten. In der Musterlösung sind teilweise mehrere Antwortmöglichkeiten angegeben. Du musst aber natürlich nur eine (richtige) Lösung aufschreiben.

Part 1

1 MARTIN: Hello. Um, I'd like a single to Aberdeen, please.
TICKETSELLER: OK. Leaving today?
MARTIN: If possible, yes. I think there's one that goes at ten past nine.
TICKETSELLER: Yes, that's right but I'm afraid there's a short delay today because of
5   heavy traffic on the M4 coming in to London.
MARTIN: Oh. OK.
TICKETSELLER: At the moment we're looking at about 15 minutes. So it'll be just
    before nine thirty before you get away.
MARTIN: That's fine. I've got a coach card.
10 TICKETSELLER: OK. Let's have a look. Right. Have you got any additional luggage?
MARTIN: No, just this one bag.
TICKETSELLER: OK. That's ... er ... £42.50.
MARTIN: Oh, wow. So much? Even with a coach card?
TICKETSELLER: Well, the 'walk-up' fares are always the most expensive. That
15   means if you want to leave right away, you'll have to pay more. But do you
    have to go today? Because if you book in advance, it's much cheaper.
MARTIN: Oh. OK. No, I'm not in a rush.
TICKETSELLER: Well, if you wait a day or two and book online, you can probably
    save another 30 per cent.
20 MARTIN: OK. Thanks. I can leave tomorrow. Thank you very much for your
    help ...

1. (at) **ten past nine/9.10**
* Hinweis: Z. 3

2. (because of) (heavy) **traffic**
   Hinweis: *Z. 4 f.*

3. (just before) **9.30**/(about) **15 min**(utes) **later**/(at) **9.25**
   Hinweis: *Z. 7 f.*

4. (just) **one** (piece/bag)
   Hinweis: *Z. 10 f.*

5. (£) **42.50**
   Hinweis: *Z. 12*

6. (another) **30 per cent/30 %**
   Hinweis: *Z. 18 f.*

Part 2

1 COACH DRIVER: Good morning. I'm John, your driver today. Before we leave, I'd
like to apologise for our late departure from London this morning. We're
about 20 minutes late at the moment but if everything goes well we should be
able to make that up by around lunchtime.

5 I'd also like to apologise for some problems we're experiencing on this coach
at the moment. As you can tell, it's very warm in here and that's because the
air conditioning's not working properly. There's also a problem with the Wi-
Fi and that's why there's no Internet available. However, we do have some
good news. When we get to Luton there's going to be a change of driver but

10 we're also going to change the coach. So after Luton everything should be back
to normal again.
Finally, I'd like to remind you to fasten your safety belts and to make sure your
luggage is not blocking the aisle.
So, let's get on the way. Relax and enjoy the view. Thank you.

15 If you have any questions, please ...

Hinweis: *Jeder in dieser Aufgabe vorgegebene Satz enthält einen inhaltlichen Fehler.*
Folge dem Text also aufmerksam und finde das Wort im Satz, das nicht mit dem
Hörtext übereinstimmt. Schreibe das richtige Wort aus dem Hörtext auf.

1. We're about ~~half an hour~~ late.
                20 minutes
   Hinweis: *Z. 2 f.*

2. We ~~won't~~ be able to make that up by around lunchtime.
   should

   Hinweis: *Z. 3 f.*

3. The ~~heating~~'s not working properly.
   air conditioning

   Hinweis: *Z. 6 f.*

4. There's no ~~on-board service~~ available.
   Internet/Wi-Fi

   Hinweis: *Z. 7 f.*

5. There's going to be a change of ~~tyres~~.
   driver/coach

   Hinweis: *Z. 9 f.*

Part 3

1   MARTIN: And are you going to Aberdeen, too?

   TOURIST: No, I'm getting out in Edinburgh.

   MARTIN: OK.

   TOURIST: Yeah, a friend of mine lives there and has invited me to stay with him.
5   Actually, he lives in a small place about half an hour from Edinburgh. What
       about you?

   MARTIN: I'm planning to go all the way to Aberdeen. I was thinking of going to
       the Highland Games on Saturday.

   TOURIST: Really? In Aberdeen? Have you got somewhere to stay?
10   MARTIN: No. I was thinking of trying the youth hostel there.

   TOURIST: Oh, I don't think you'll get a place there. Not now. The Games are very
       popular and everywhere will be booked out.

   MARTIN: OK. Have you got an idea what I could do?

   TOURIST: Well, the best thing would be to get a tent and go camping. I know a
15   campsite near Aberdeen. It's close to the river.

   MARTIN: Um, I'd need a sleeping bag, too.

   TOURIST: I know. But what about staying in a village close to Aberdeen? I know a
       place called Stonehaven. From there you can get a train to Aberdeen. It takes
       about 15 minutes. In fact I know a fantastic bed and breakfast place there.
20   Beachview. I can give you the website: beachview dot co dot uk.

   MARTIN: Sounds perfect. I'll write it down. What was it again?

   TOURIST: Beachview dot co dot uk.

   MARTIN: Thanks. As soon as we have access to the Internet I'll have a look at it ...

1. The American tourist is staying with a **friend** near Edinburgh.
   ✐ Hinweis: Z. 4

2. The American thinks the youth hostels in Aberdeen will be **booked out/full**.
   ✐ Hinweis: Z. 11 f.

3. Martin would need a **tent/sleeping bag** for camping.
   ✐ Hinweis: Z. 14 ff.

4. Stonehaven is a **village/place** close to Aberdeen.
   ✐ Hinweis: Z. 17 f.

5. In Stonehaven Martin could stay at a **bed and breakfast** (place)/**B and B/
   B & B/B + B**.
   ✐ Hinweis: Z. 19

Part 4

1 GUIDE: Well, I think you know about the bagpiping competition. There are mass-
ed band competitions but there are solo piping competitions as well. But here
are four more competitions I'd like to tell you about.
The first competition is the weight throw. The weights are made of metal.
5 There's a chain with a handle on the end attached to the weight. The winner is
the person who throws the weight the greatest distance, using one hand only.
The second competition is called "sheaf toss". A "sheaf" is a sack full of straw.
It weighs about 10 kilos. To "toss" means to throw, but you don't throw the
sack of straw as far as you can, you throw it up and over a bar. Not with your
10 hands. You have to use a pitchfork!
The third competition is "tossing the caber". A caber is a tree trunk. It's about
5 metres long. You hold the caber at the bottom and toss it, or throw it, so it
turns over in the air and lands on the ground. Of course, the heavier the caber
the harder it is to throw it into the air.
15 A final competition I can tell you about is called "tug of war". Two teams stand
at different ends of a long rope and pull as hard as they can. The team that
pulls the other team four metres off the middle is the winner.
Of course there are other …

✐ **Hinweis:** *Sieh dir bei jeder Aufgabe die Bilderfolge genau an, denn die Bilder unter-*
✐ *scheiden sich nur in Einzelheiten. Damit du das richtige Bild findest, solltest du beim*
✐ *Hörtext auch auf feine Unterschiede achten, z. B. ob das Wurfgeschoss mit einer*
✐ *oder aber mit beiden Händen gehalten wird.*

1. Weight throw

☐ ✓ ☐ ☐

✎ **Hinweis:** *Z. 4 ff.*

2. Sheaf toss

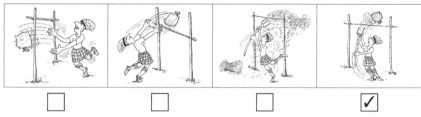

☐ ☐ ☐ ✓

✎ **Hinweis:** *Z. 7 ff.; pitchfork = Heugabel*

3. Tossing the caber

☐ ☐ ✓ ☐

✎ **Hinweis:** *Z. 11 ff.*

4. Tug of war

✓ ☐ ☐ ☐

✎ **Hinweis:** *Z. 15 ff.*

B Use of English

Allgemeiner Hinweis: In diesem Prüfungsteil musst du dein Wissen im Bereich Wortschatz, Grammatik und Rechtschreibung unter Beweis stellen.

Aufgabe 1

Hinweis: Diese Aufgabe testet deinen Wortschatz und deine Grammatikkenntnisse. Achte auch auf die korrekte Rechtschreibung der gesuchten Wörter.

Lücke:

(1) „more <u>than</u>" = „mehr <u>als</u>"

(4) „to be famous <u>for</u>" = „berühmt sein <u>für</u>"

(5) Hier kannst du entweder das modale Hilfsverb „can" einsetzen oder auch das „will-future" verwenden.

(6) Frage mit „to be" im „simple present": "Are you interested in . . .?" = „Bist du/ Sind Sie an . . . interessiert?"

Scotland is (0) **part** of the United Kingdom. More (1) **than** five million people live there. Edinburgh, its capital, is the second largest (2) **city/town**. Aberdeen is called Europe's oil capital (3) **because/as/since/for** Scotland has the largest oil reserves in the European Union. Scotland is famous (4) **for** its lakes and mountains. All year round you (5) **can/will** find lots of tourists travelling the country. So, (6) **are** you interested in visiting Scotland?

Aufgabe 2

Hinweis: Hier werden verschiedene Grammatikbereiche überprüft, z. B. die Bildung der Zeiten und die Steigerung von Adjektiven. Bei größeren Unsicherheiten empfiehlt sich die Wiederholung des jeweiligen Themas mithilfe der Kurzgrammatik, die du im Trainingsband findest.

(1) Steigerung des Adjektivs „big": big – bigger – biggest. Beachte auch die Mitlautverdopplung „big/biggest".

(2) countri<u>es</u>: Mehrzahl des Nomens „country". Achte auf die Rechtschreibung: aus „-y" wird „-ie".

(3) „went": Zeitform „simple past"; Signalwort „<u>last</u> August"

(4) „didn't stay": Zeitform „simple past", bezieht sich auch auf „last August"; hier ist das Verb zusätzlich verneint: „did not/didn't"

(5) „gett<u>ing</u>": die „ing"-Form folgt nach „like", wenn man etwas allgemein gerne tut.

(6) Aufgrund des Signalworts „next year" muss hier eine Form stehen, die ein zukünftiges Ereignis ausdrückt; in diesem Fall kannst du sowohl das „will-future" als auch das „going-to future" oder das „present progressive" verwenden.

Thousands of (0 tourist) **tourists** go to Edinburgh every year to experience the Festival. The Edinburgh Festival is one of the (1 big) **biggest** events in Scotland. People from Scotland and many other (2 country) **countries** go there. Last August Tim (3 go) **went** there for the first time. He (4 not stay) **didn't stay** long but he enjoyed it. Tim likes (5 get) **getting** to know different cultures. That's why he (6 fly) **will fly/is going to fly/is flying** to the USA next year.

Aufgabe 3

Hinweis: Hier werden dein Wortschatz und v. a. deine Grammatikkenntnisse getestet. Jede Aufgabe lenkt dein Augenmerk auf vier unterstrichene Stellen im Satz, wovon eine Stelle fehlerhaft ist. Den sprachlichen Fehler gilt es zu entdecken und zu markieren. Es wird nicht erwartet, dass du den Fehler erklärst oder berichtigst. Solltest du bei dieser Aufgabe Schwierigkeiten haben, empfiehlt sich ein Blick in die Kurzgrammatik des Trainingsbandes.

1. On Monday I climbed Ben Nevis, the most high mountain in Great Britain.
     A   B   ⓒ   D

   Hinweis: Fehler bei der Steigerung des Adjektivs „high". Da es sich um ein einsilbiges Adjektiv handelt, lautet die richtige Steigerung „highest". (vgl. die Kurzgrammatik im Trainingsband, Kapitel 12)

2. On the way down I fell and ruined my jeans but I didn't hurt me.
               A B   C   ⓓ

   Hinweis: Fehler bei der Auswahl des Fürwortes (Pronomens). Die richtige Lösung ist das rückbezügliche Fürwort „myself" (vgl. Kurzgrammatik, Kapitel 3).

3. The next day I met a man which showed me how to play the bagpipes.
       A   B   ⓒ   D

   Hinweis: Fehler bei der Wahl des Relativpronomens. Die richtige Lösung lautet „who", weil hier auf eine Person („a man") Bezug genommen wird (vgl. Kurzgrammatik, Kapitel 11)

4. The weather has been really good so far: sunny and warm all time.
     A   B   C   ⓓ

   Hinweis: Hier müsste es richtig heißen: „all of the time"

5. The best thing is: I <u>haven't met</u> <u>some</u> unfriendly peo<u>ple</u>. <u>Everybody</u> is nice.

          A   (**B**)   **C**   **D**

Hinweis: *Fehler bei der Verwendung von „some/any". Da der Satz durch „haven't" verneint ist, muss „**any**" verwendet werden. „Some" verwendet man in bejahten Sätzen.*

6. If they speak <u>slow</u>, I <u>can</u> even understand <u>their</u> Scottish <u>accent</u>.

          (**A**)   **B**   **C**   **D**

Hinweis: *Fehler bei der Unterscheidung von Adverb und Adjektiv. In diesem Satz wird das Adverb „**slowly**" benötigt, da das Verb „speak" näher beschrieben wird: <u>Auf welche Art und Weise</u> sprechen sie?*

7. At the moment I'm <u>at</u> the railway station. <u>I'm waiting of</u> my train <u>to</u> Edinburgh.

                  A   **B** (**C**)   **D**

Hinweis: *Richtig ist die Wortverbindung „waiting <u>for</u>" für „warten <u>auf</u>".*

8. <u>I'm looking forward</u> <u>to</u> Edinburgh. <u>There are</u> so <u>much</u> things to see there!

        A   **B**   **C**   (**D**)

Hinweis: *Fehler bei der Unterscheidung von „much/many". Man verwendet hier „**many**", weil das Namenwort (Nomen) „things" zählbar ist. Dies erkennst du daran, dass es von „thing" auch die Mehrzahlform („things") gibt. „Much" verwendet man bei Nomen, die <u>nicht</u> zählbar sind und somit auch keine Mehrzahlform haben, z. B. „much money".*

C Reading Comprehension

Allgemeiner Hinweis: *Nach dem ersten Lesen solltest du den Inhalt des Textes im Wesentlichen verstanden haben. Bei der Bearbeitung der Aufgaben ist es nötig, dass du zunächst diejenigen Textstellen findest, auf die sich die Aufgaben beziehen. Lies diese noch einmal durch, bevor du die Lösungen aufschreibst. Die folgende Vokabelliste ist bewusst umfangreich gehalten. In der Prüfung solltest du aus Zeitgründen aber nur die Wörter nachschlagen, die du zum Verständnis des Textes unbedingt brauchst.*

Vokabelhinweise:
Z. 1: to take part in: teilnehmen an
Z. 1 f.: practice session: Übungseinheit, Trainingseinheit
Z. 4: to race: hier: ein Rennen fahren
Z. 6: profession: Beruf
Z. 6: dominated by: dominiert, beherrscht von
Z. 8: competitive: leistungsorientiert, immer der/die Beste sein wollend
Z. 10: to realise: begreifen, erkennen
Z. 16: championship: Meisterschaft

Z. 20: *close links to: enge Verbindungen zu*
Z. 21: *development driver: Testfahrer/in*
Z. 23: *to be in a rush: in Eile sein*
Z. 25: *skill: Fähigkeit, Fertigkeit*
Z. 26: *physical strength: körperliche Kraft*
Z. 26 f.: *tight corners: enge Kurven*
Z. 27: *at high speeds: bei hoher Geschwindigkeit*
Z. 28: *to compete with sb: gegen jmd. antreten, mit jmd. konkurrieren*
Z. 32: *engineer: Ingenieur/in*
Z. 32: *equipment: Ausrüstung*
Z. 34: *to be scared: Angst haben*
Z. 37: *fear: Angst*
Z. 38: *failure: Versagen*
Z. 39: *impatient: ungeduldig*

Aufgabe 1

/ **Hinweis:** *Wenn du die Überschriften richtig zuordnest, zeigt dies, dass du den Inhalt*
/ *des Textes im Wesentlichen verstanden hast.*
/ *Vokabeln:*
/ *athletic: athletisch, trainiert, fit*
/ *charity events: Wohltätigkeitsveranstaltungen*
/ *race course: Rennstrecke*
/ *successes: Erfolge*

paragraph 1 (lines 1–6)	B
paragraph 2 (lines 7–13)	D
paragraph 3 (lines 14–18)	F
paragraph 4 (lines 19–24)	G
paragraph 5 (lines 25–33)	A
paragraph 6 (lines 34–40)	E

Aufgabe 2

1. in her teens
   Hinweis: *Z. 10 f.; when = wann, unusual = ungewöhnlich*

2. (they met) in her dad's (motorbike) shop
   Hinweis: *Z. 12 f.; how = wie, to get to know each other = sich kennenlernen*

3. (her) husband/Toto Wolff
   Hinweis: *Z. 19 f.; who = wer, connections = Kontakte, Verbindungen*

4. head and neck
   Hinweis: *Z. 26 ff.; which = hier: welche (Körperteile), pressure = Druck*

5. She's careful about what she eats. / She trains for two hours every day.
   Hinweis: *Z. 30 f.; what = was, in order to = um ... zu*

Aufgabe 3

	line or lines
1.	8
2.	15/16
3.	22/23
4.	25/26
5.	35/36

Aufgabe 4

Hinweis: *Bei dieser Aufgabe werden dir englische Wörter vorgegeben, die im Text vorkommen, sowie jeweils vier verschiedene Möglichkeiten, das Wort ins Deutsche zu übersetzen. Die Angaben in Klammern sind grammatikalische Zusatzinformationen, die dir helfen können, die richtige Antwort zu finden. Lies dir zunächst im Lesetext den gesamten Satz durch, der das betreffende Wort enthält. Nun hast du verschiedene Möglichkeiten vorzugehen:*
Übersetze den Satz aus dem Text ins Deutsche und kreuze das richtige Wort an oder setze jedes angegebene deutsche Wort für das englische Wort in den Text ein. Beim Übersetzen wirst du schnell herausfinden, ob die jeweilige Bedeutung im Satzzusammenhang einen Sinn ergibt oder nicht.

1. time (line 4)

   ☐ Zeit *(Nomen)*

   ☑ Mal *(Nomen)*

   ☐ stoppen *(Verb + Obj.)*

   ☐ einen geeigneten Zeitpunkt wählen *(Verb + Obj.)*

   Hinweis: *Das letzte <u>Mal</u>, dass dies eine Frau tat, war 1975, als Lella Lombardi, eine italienische Fahrerin, in Südafrika ein Rennen fuhr.*

2. turn (line 22)

   ☐ wenden, umdrehen *(Verb + Obj.)*

   ☐ abbiegen *(Verb)*

   ☑ werden *(Verb ohne Obj.)*

   ☐ Kurve, Biegung *(Nomen)*

   Hinweis: *Im Dezember dieses Jahres <u>wird</u> Susie 33 Jahre alt.*

3. mean (line 26)

   ☑ bedeuten *(Verb + Obj.)*

   ☐ meinen *(Verb)*

   ☐ geizig *(Adj.)*

   ☐ gemein *(Adj.)*

   Hinweis: *Was <u>bedeutet</u> das für einen Rennfahrer/eine Rennfahrerin?*

4. light (line 31)

- [ ] Licht *(Nomen)*
- [ ] anzünden *(Verb + Obj.)*
- [ ] erleuchten *(Verb + Obj.)*
- [x] leicht *(Adj.)*

Hinweis: *Sie ist klein und <u>leicht</u>, und in der Formel 1 ist das von Vorteil.*

5. like (line 35)

- [ ] mögen *(Verb + Obj.)*
- [ ] möchten *(Verb + Obj.)*
- [x] wie *(Präp.)*
- [ ] also *(Adv.) (umgs)*

Hinweis: <u>Wie</u> *alle Formel 1-Fahrer kennt sie die Risiken.*

D Text Production

Allgemeiner Hinweis: *Entscheide dich <u>entweder</u> für die E-Mail <u>oder</u> für die Bildergeschichte. Du darfst ein zweisprachiges Wörterbuch verwenden. Beachte die Vorgaben zu Umfang, Form und Inhalt, die in der Aufgabenstellung beschrieben sind. Die Lösungsbeispiele sind bewusst etwas länger gehalten, sodass du verschiedene Ideen für deine eigene Lösung bekommst.*

1. Correspondence: E-Mail

Hinweis: *Lies dir die Aufgabenstellung genau durch und versetze dich in die beschriebene Situation. Bei Alex handelt es sich vermutlich um einen etwa gleichaltrigen Schüler/eine gleichaltrige Schülerin, zu dem/der du im Rahmen eines Austauschprogramms einen ersten Kontakt herstellen möchtest. Du schreibst also eine persönliche E-Mail, die mit keinen besonderen Anforderungen an die Form verbunden ist (wie das z.B. bei einer Bewerbung nötig wäre). Vergiss dennoch nicht, eine Anrede und eine passende Verabschiedung mit Angabe deines Namens einzufügen. Gehe in deiner E-Mail auf die Punkte ein, die in der Aufgabenstellung angegeben sind. Manchmal kannst du auch auswählen oder selbst entscheiden, über was du in deiner E-Mail schreiben möchtest. Gehe aber auf jeden Fall auf alle geforderten Punkte der Reihe nach ein.*

Hi Alex,

How are you? I'm writing to introduce myself. My name is Michael and I'm in the ninth grade of your German partner school. I'm really looking forward to visiting you in July! I think it will be interesting to meet you and be at your school – and it will be great to practise my English.

Do you do a lot of sports at your school? That would be great because I'm quite a sporty guy. I love playing football and tennis.

How many kids are in our class? What do you usually do in your free time?

I hope there will be time to visit some places in Scotland – do you think we could go to Loch Ness together? Or are there other places you would suggest? Do you have any ideas what we could do in the evenings?

I also wanted to ask if I will have my own room while I'm staying at your place.

Before I forget it, I wanted to tell you that I have a gluten allergy, which means that I can only eat bread or pasta that is gluten-free, but I eat all other foods.

I hope you are fine and I'm looking forward to hearing from you!

Best wishes, Michael   *(209 words)*

2. Creative Writing: Picture Story

Hinweis: In der Aufgabenstellung findest du bereits den Titel der Geschichte ("The Scottish castle ghost"), eine kurze Einleitung ("Last summer ...") sowie fünf Bilder. Betrachte sie ganz genau, um den Inhalt der Geschichte zu verstehen. Überlege dir zu jedem Bild, was du dazu schreiben könntest und überlege dir Formulierungen auf Englisch. Beschreibe dann die Handlung der Geschichte von Bild zu Bild. Gliedere deinen Text in Absätze. Lies dir am Ende alles noch einmal durch: Ist deine Geschichte verständlich? Hast du den Witz der Geschichte erfasst (ein echtes Gespenst erscheint und Callum erschreckt sich selbst)?

The Scottish castle ghost

Last summer Callum and his class visited an old Scottish castle. A friendly guide showed them suits of armour and pictures of people who had lived in the castle hundreds of years ago. While the other pupils were listening to the guide, Callum secretly pulled a ghost costume out of his bag and put it on. Then he shouted "Huuuuu" and waved his arms at his classmates. Everyone was terribly frightened and ran away.

"That trick really worked," Callum said to himself smiling. But he couldn't enjoy the moment for long because suddenly a real ghost appeared and Callum was completely shocked himself! Maybe the ghost wanted to teach Callum a lesson not to frighten other people.   *(121 words)*

E 2015-13

Notenschlüssel

Notenstufen	1	2	3	4	5	6
Punkte	80–68	67–55	54–41	40–27	26–13	12–0

A Listening

✏ **Allgemeiner Hinweis:** *Es werden vier kurze Hörtexte von der CD vorgespielt. Dein Hörverständnis wird dann mittels der zugehörigen Aufgaben überprüft: Task 1 bezieht sich auf Part 1, Task 2 auf Part 2, usw. Lies die Aufgaben zuerst genau durch. So erkennst du, auf welche Informationen du dich beim Hören des jeweiligen Textes besonders konzentrieren solltest. Löse dann während des Zuhörens oder in der Pause im Anschluss die Aufgaben. Die Hörtexte werden zwei Mal vorgespielt. Im Prüfungsteil Listening Comprehension erhältst du für Rechtschreibfehler keinen Punktabzug, solange deine Lösung noch als inhaltlich richtig erkannt werden kann.*

Part 1

1 EMPLOYEE: Good afternoon, Stratford tourist office. Wendy Taylor speaking. How can I help you?

MR THOMPSON: Hello, Peter Thompson here. I'm going on a holiday in Europe later this year. My son and me, we're thinking about spending two or three

5 days in Stratford.

EMPLOYEE: That sounds great.

MR THOMPSON: Yes, ... well, ... you see, we're not sure if there's enough to see and do in Stratford if we stay that long.

EMPLOYEE: Well, since this is the anniversary year, there are even more events

10 than usual.

MR THOMPSON: Anniversary?

EMPLOYEE: Well, you know that Stratford is the hometown of William Shakespeare, the well-known playwright ...

MR THOMPSON: Of course I do.

15 EMPLOYEE: ... and he died in sixteen-hundred and sixteen, exactly 400 years ago.

MR THOMPSON: So are there any special events in Stratford this year?

EMPLOYEE: Unfortunately you missed the great parade on 23rd April, that's Shakespeare's birthday and also the day he died. But there are celebrations all year. And there are some special historical walks with a guide who explains

20 what the town was like in Shakespeare's time. And of course the usual sightseeing tours.

MR THOMPSON: Could you send me some information about the special anniversary events, please?

EMPLOYEE: Of course, but you can also find them on our website at shakespearean-
25   niversary.co.uk.
MR THOMPSON: Can I make reservations online, too?
EMPLOYEE: Yes, you will find booking forms on our website.
MR THOMPSON: OK. Thank you very much. You've been very helpful.
EMPLOYEE: You are welcome, Mr Thompson. Goodbye.
30   MR THOMPSON: Goodbye.

✏ **Hinweis:** *Finde in jedem Satz die falsche Information und ersetze diese durch die richtige Angabe aus dem Hörtext.*

1. We're thinking about spending two or three ~~weeks~~ **days** in Stratford.
   ✏ Hinweis: *Z. 5*

2. There are even more ~~tourists~~ **events** than usual.
   ✏ Hinweis: *Z. 9*

3. William Shakespeare died in ~~1600~~ **1616**.
   ✏ Hinweis: *Z. 15*

4. You missed the great parade on ~~3rd~~ **23rd** April.
   ✏ Hinweis: *Z. 17*

5. Find them on our website at shakespeareanniversary.~~com~~ **co.uk**
   ✏ Hinweis: *Z. 24 f.*

Part 2

1   GUIDE: ... and we've already arrived at our next stop. Ladies and Gentlemen, the
     famous Royal Shakespeare Theatre! Here you can see many of Shakespeare's
     plays live on stage. The building you are looking at is actually about 70 years
     old. After some years of renovation it reopened again in 2010. In fact there are
5   two theatres here.
     The Royal Shakespeare Theatre has about 1,000 seats. And the Swan Theatre
     at the back of the building is about half that size.
     The ticket counters are open for another hour today, so if you are interested in
     seeing a play, you can buy some tickets while we're here. Several different
10   plays by Shakespeare are currently in the programme: Romeo and Juliet, Ham-
     let and A Midsummer Night's Dream.
     Enjoy your time here. And don't forget, we move on at 4.30. The final stop of
     our tour is Holy Trinity Church. There, we'll visit Shakespeare's grave. *(fading)*
     And by the way, did you know that Shakespeare rarely ...

1. B (Z. 2f.)
2. D (Z. 4)
3. E (Z. 6f.; „half that size" = halb so groß)
4. I (Z. 13)

1	2	3	4
B	D	E	I

Part 3

1 MAN: Good afternoon. Can I help you?

    ROBERT: Good afternoon. I'm in Stratford this week and I'd like to see *Romeo and Juliet*. Are there any seats available?

    MAN: Let me see. Do you want to see an afternoon or an evening performance?

5 ROBERT: Evening, please.

    MAN: Well, Tuesday is fully booked and an the two following days we are showing *Hamlet*.

    ROBERT: Oh dear, and we leave an Friday.

    MAN: Well, there are seats for the afternoon performance on Wednesday at 4.15.

10 ROBERT: Yes, that would be OK.

    MAN: We have tickets in the circle for £ 25 and in the upper circle for £ 35 or £ 40.

    ROBERT: Oh, that's rather expensive.

    MAN: Well, how old are you?

15 ROBERT: I'm 16.

    MAN: Great, then we can offer you a discount ticket for £ 15.

    ROBERT: Fantastic. Can I book two tickets for the circle?

    MAN: Two tickets?

    ROBERT: Yes, I want to come with my father.

20 MAN: I see. He'll have to pay the full price, I'm afraid. That'll be £ 40 for the two of you.

    ROBERT: Yes, all right. Do I have to pay now?

    MAN: Either that or you can pick up your tickets on Wednesday and pay then. But you'll have to do that at least one hour before the performance starts.

25 ROBERT: That's fine.

    MAN: Then I will reserve the tickets for you … in the name of …?

    ROBERT: Thompson, Robert Thompson.

MAN: OK, two tickets are reserved for you in row D in the circle for the performance of *Romeo and Juliet* on Wednesday afternoon.
30 ROBERT: Thank you very much. Goodbye.
MAN: Goodbye.

✏ **Hinweis:** *Ergänze die fehlenden Angaben im Formular.*

1. Wednesday
   ✏ **Hinweis:** *Z. 9*

2. 4.15 (pm)
   ✏ **Hinweis:** *Z. 9*

3. 1/one
   ✏ **Hinweis:** *Z. 16–20*

4. 40
   ✏ **Hinweis:** *Z. 20 f.*

5. one hour before (the performance/show starts) / 3.15 (pm)
   ✏ **Hinweis:** *Z. 23 f.*

6. D (in the circle)
   ✏ **Hinweis:** *Z. 28 f.*

Part 4

1 WAITRESS: Are you ready to order now?
MR THOMPSON: Well, not quite, I'm afraid.
WAITRESS: Perhaps I can get you something to drink?
MR THOMPSON: Yes, that's a good idea. What would you like to drink, Robert?
5 ROBERT: A coke, please.
WAITRESS: And for you, sir?
MR THOMPSON: I'd like some water, please.
WAITRESS: OK, thank you. I'll be right back.
MR THOMPSON: So, Robert, would you like to have a starter? How about the soup
10 of the day?
ROBERT: What sort of soup is it?
MR THOMPSON: Vegetable, I think.
ROBERT: Hmm, …
MR THOMPSON: Or would you prefer a tuna salad?
15 ROBERT: I think I'll have the Caesar's salad.
MR THOMPSON: Well, I'll go for the soup, I think. And what about a main course?
ROBERT: I don't really like fish.

MR THOMPSON: Well, the beef steak sounds very nice, doesn't it?

ROBERT: Only if it is well-done. Otherwise I'll take something else.

20 MR THOMPSON: We'll ask the waitress then. And which vegetables do you want
   to have?

ROBERT: I'll have the roast potatoes.

MR THOMPSON: It seems they've only got them baked or mashed.

ROBERT: Then I'll have mashed potatoes and carrots. And what about you?

25 MR THOMPSON: I'm having the grilled fish, baked potatoes and peas. And an apple
   pie for dessert.

ROBERT: And I'll have the toffee surprise rather than the lemon tart.

WAITRESS: Here are your drinks. A coke for you, … and a mineral water for you,
   sir. Can I take your order now?

30 MR THOMPSON: Is the beef steak well-done?

WAITRESS: As you wish, you can have it well-done, if you like.

MR THOMPSON: Good, in that case we would like to have one well-done beef
   steak with …

✎ **Hinweis:** *In diesem Dialog erfährst du, was sich Robert (R) und sein Vater (F) als Vorspeise, Hauptgericht, Beilage und zum Nachtisch bestellen. Trage jeweils das Namenskürzel (R oder F) in die Kästchen ein.*

1. Ceasar's Salad $\boxed{\text{R}}$

   Vegetable Soup $\boxed{\text{F}}$

   ✎ **Hinweis:** *Robert: Z. 15, Father: Z. 16*

2. Grilled Fish $\boxed{\text{F}}$

   Beef Steak $\boxed{\text{R}}$

   ✎ **Hinweis:** *Robert: Z. 18 f./32, Father: Z. 25*

3. Baked Potatoes $\boxed{\text{F}}$

   Mashed Potatoes $\boxed{\text{R}}$

   ✎ **Hinweis:** *Robert: Z. 24, Father: Z. 25*

4. Carrots $\boxed{\text{R}}$

   Peas $\boxed{\text{F}}$

   ✎ **Hinweis:** *Robert: Z. 24, Father: Z. 25*

5. Apple Pie $\boxed{\text{F}}$

   Toffee Surprise $\boxed{\text{R}}$

   ✎ **Hinweis:** *Robert: Z. 27, Father: Z. 25 f.*

B Use of English

✔ **Allgemeiner Hinweis:** *In diesem Prüfungsteil musst du dein Wissen im Bereich Wortschatz, Grammatik und Rechtschreibung unter Beweis stellen.*

Aufgabe 1

✔ **Hinweis:** *Schreibe das Wort in der Klammer in der richtigen Form in die Lücke, sodass es sich korrekt in den vorgegebenen Satz einfügt. Anbei findest du eine Zuordnung der Lösungen zum jeweiligen Grammatikbereich. Solltest du bei der Bearbeitung dieser Aufgabe Schwierigkeiten gehabt haben, empfiehlt es sich, das jeweilige Grammatikthema nochmals in der Kurzgrammatik zu wiederholen.*

1 most important: Steigerung und Vergleich
2 don't have/haven't had: Zeiten (Simple present/Present perfect)
3 does: Zeiten/Fragen mit to do-Umschreibung im Simple present
4 includes: Zeiten (Simple present)
5 healthy/healthier: Adjektive/Steigerung und Vergleich
6 (prefer) having/to have: -ing-Form oder Infinitiv nach bestimmten Verben
7 European: Adjektive Länder/Kontinente
8 has existed: Zeiten (Present perfect)
9 quickly: Adverbien der Art und Weise
10 will change/is going to change: Zeiten (Aussagen über die Zukunft)

People have different ideas and (0 opinion) **opinions** about breakfast. Some people say it is the (1 important) **most important** meal of the day. Statistics show that people who (2 not have) **don't have/haven't had** breakfast often have problems with concentration and health. England is known for its cooked breakfast; but what (3 do) **does** this full English breakfast consist of? A typical English breakfast (4 include) **includes** eggs, either poached or scrambled, with bacon and sausages, followed by toast with marmalade. A (5 health) **healthy/healthier** version is just one egg and some toast. Whereas in Europe, especially in Germany, people prefer (6 have) **having/to have** cheese, ham, eggs and some bread as a start to the day, nearly all the southern (7 Europe) **European** countries tend to have only coffee and some bread or pastries. The tradition of the English breakfast (8 exist) **has existed** for many years, and visitors, hotel guests and people who have the time still enjoy it to this day. However, in our hectic and health-conscious world, many English people prefer a continental breakfast or they (9 quick) **quickly** get something to eat and drink on their way to work. It is likely that in future our culture of eating (10 change) **will change/is going to change** even more. The full English breakfast may soon be a thing of the past.

Aufgabe 2

✎ **Hinweis:** *Bei dieser anspruchsvollen Aufgabe ist dir kein Wort vorgegeben, sondern du musst selbst ein Wort finden, das in den Satzzusammenhang passt.*

1 *from* China: <u>aus</u> China
2 *in* <u>every</u> street: in <u>jeder</u> Straße
3 *to put/pour:* geben, gießen
4 *so that they did/would not break:* damit sie nicht zerbrachen, zerbrechen würden
5 <u>at</u> 4 o'clock: <u>um</u> 4 Uhr
6 *others/some/many:* andere/einige/viele
7 *that/which:* hier Relativpronomen: die, welche
8 *have closed (Present perfect):* haben zugemacht
9 *for example/for instance:* zum Beispiel
10 *there is:* es gibt

Since the 18th (0) **century** the United Kingdom has been one of the world's greatest tea consumers. At first, tea was mainly imported (1) **from** China. In those days it was sold in almost (2) **every** street in London. People at that time called it 'China drink'. Not only tea but also small porcelain tea cups were shipped to Europe. These cups were so thin that it was necessary to (3) **put/pour** some milk in first, so that they (4) **did/would** not break when the hot tea went in. People still use these porcelain cups now and then for special occasions. Even today people in England add milk to their tea and some sugar, depending on their taste. In Britain the word 'tea' describes both a hot drink and a light meal in the afternoon (5) **at** about four o'clock. For some people it is their last meal of the day, for (6) **others/some/many** a snack between lunch and dinner. In many towns and cities in Britain there are tea rooms (7) **that/which** serve tea and other drinks. But since the 1950s many tea rooms (8) **have** closed. Today people prefer health-orientated drinks, for (9) **example/instance** fruit or herbal teas. Nevertheless, (10) **there** is no other country in Europe where people drink more tea.

C Reading Comprehension

✎ **Allgemeiner Hinweis:** *In diesem Prüfungsteil darfst du ein Wörterbuch (aber kein elektronisches) verwenden. Lies dir den Text durch und versuche ihn grob zu verstehen. Markiere auch unbekannte Wörter. Beim zweiten Durchgang sollte dein Ziel sein, den Text genau zu verstehen. Schlage hierzu die markierten Wörter im Wörterbuch nach, die du zum detaillierten Textverständnis benötigst. Beginne anschließend mit der Bearbeitung der Aufgaben. Verwende auch hier bei sprachlichen Unklarheiten das Wörterbuch, damit du die Aufgabenstellung verstehst.*

Vokabelhinweise:

Z. 1: *vinegar: Essig*
Z. 9: *deep-fried: frittiert*
Z. 9: *batter: Panade*
Z. 9: *flour: Mehl*
Z. 17: *rationed: rationiert, nur in begrenzter Menge erhältlich*
Z. 19: *filling: hier: sättigend*
Z. 22: *posh: vornehm, fein*
Z. 30: *nowadays: heutzutage*
Z. 32: *fake: hier: nachgemacht, (einer Zeitung) nachempfunden*
Z. 36: *valuable source: wertvolle Quelle*
Z. 39: *physically: körperlich, hier auch: für den Körper*
Z. 39: *mentally: seelisch, hier auch: für die Seele*
Kasten:
flour (self-raising): Mehl mit Backpulverzusatz
to boil: in Wasser kochen
to sprinkle: träufeln
ingredient: Zutat
bowl: Schüssel

Aufgabe 1

✎ **Hinweis:** *Der Lesetext ist in Absätze (paragraphs A–F) gegliedert. Ordne jedem dieser Absätze jeweils die passende Überschrift zu. Drei Überschriften stimmen inhaltlich nicht mit dem Lesetext überein.*

Vokabelhinweis:
occasion: Anlass

paragraph B	paragraph C	paragraph D	paragraph E	paragraph F
7	6	3	2	4

Aufgabe 2

🖊 **Hinweis:** *Beantworte die Fragen anhand des Lesetextes. Du kannst in Stichpunkten antworten.*

1. flour, salt, (sparkling) water, beer
   🖊 **Hinweis:** *Abschnitt B, im Kasten: "For the batter"*
2. (the) Spanish
   🖊 **Hinweis:** *Z. 12 f.*
3. (because it was) cheap (and) filling
   🖊 **Hinweis:** *Z. 17 ff.*
4. (it) kept (the) food warm
   🖊 **Hinweis:** *Z. 29 f.*
5. plastic
   🖊 **Hinweis:** *Z. 32 f.*

Aufgabe 3

🖊 **Hinweis:** *Hier musst du notieren, wo die angegebenen Informationen im Lesetext zu finden sind. Gib dabei jeweils die Zeilen an.*

	line or lines
1.	22–23
2.	25–26
3.	31–32
4.	34
5.	36

Aufgabe 4

🖊 **Hinweis:** *Von den Aussagen b–j decken sich nur fünf mit dem Inhalt des Lesetextes. Vergleiche die Aussagen mit den Informationen aus dem Lesetext, wähle die richtigen Aussagen aus und notiere diese.*

1. c
   🖊 **Hinweis:** *Z. 8 f., sowie Kasten vorletzte Zeile*

2. e

✒ Hinweis: Abschnitt B, Kasten: vorletzte und letzte Zeile

3. f

✒ Hinweis: Z. 14 ff.

4. i

✒ Hinweis: Z. 23

5. j

✒ Hinweis: Z. 35 f.

D Text Production

✒ **Allgemeiner Hinweis:** *Entscheide dich <u>entweder</u> für die E-Mail <u>oder</u> für die Bildergeschichte. Du darfst ein zweisprachiges Wörterbuch verwenden. Beachte die Vorgaben zu Umfang, Form und Inhalt. Die Lösungsbeispiele sind jedoch etwas länger gehalten, sodass du verschiedene Ideen für deine eigene Lösung bekommst.*

1. Correspondence: E-Mail

✒ **Hinweis:** *Schreibe eine E-Mail an Carmen <u>oder</u> José. Was den Inhalt deiner E-Mail betrifft, so erhältst du in der Aufgabe bereits fünf Vorgaben (mit • gekennzeichnet), auf die du unbedingt eingehen musst. Diese Vorgaben darfst du selbst ausgestalten – Ideen und Beispiele, was du jeweils schreiben könntest, findest du ebenfalls in den Angaben (mit – gekennzeichnet). Vergiss nicht, in deiner E-Mail eine Anrede, eine Schlussformel sowie deinen Namen einzufügen. Die folgende E-Mail ist ein Lösungsbeispiel.*

Dear Carmen,

How are you? I hope you're fine. I'm quite happy with my English course here in Malta. My parents said I should go there. They love Malta because they met there twenty years ago at a language course. The teachers and the students at the language school are nice, but most students are German. So it's a pity that I don't speak English a lot during after-class activities. Lessons are from 9 am to 1 pm every day, with only two short breaks. After a light lunch we go to the beach or we sometimes visit historic places. Have you ever done a language course before? I've got an idea: I'd like to do another language course next summer. Could you imagine joining me? How about Ireland? We could study together and also speak English in our free time.

Best wishes,

(your name)

(146 words)

2. Creative Writing: Picture Story

✎ **Hinweis:** *Schreibe die Bildergeschichte „A new job". Der Anfang ist bereits vorgegeben. Er ist in der Zeitform „Simple past" (Hinweis: „were") verfasst – behalte also diese Zeitform auch in deinem Text bei. Erzähle, was in jedem Bild passiert und verbinde diese Informationen zu einem schlüssigen Text. Beschriftungen (z. B. „Rocky Gorilla") oder Sprechblasen (z. B. „Help!!!") verdeutlichen zum einen die Bilder und dürfen außerdem von dir direkt in deine Geschichte, z. B. als wörtliche Rede, übernommen werden. Achte darauf, dass deine Geschichte in Einleitung, Hauptteil und Schluss gegliedert ist. Der folgende Text ist ein Lösungsbeispiel.*

A new job

One morning, Mr Smith, the zoo director, and Nick, the zookeeper, were in a panic. Rocky, the gorilla, had escaped!
The two men stood in front of Rocky's cage. They saw that the door was open, and they had no clue where Rocky could be. Mr Smith had an idea: Nick should wear a gorilla costume and replace Rocky. Nick didn't like the idea at all, but he didn't have a choice. Soon he was inside the costume and hanging in Rocky's tree. The visitors didn't notice anything, but silly Nick leaned too far into Leo Lion's place. The branch Nick was sitting on broke off and he fell on the floor, in front of Leo's feet, and screamed "Help!!!" Instead of attacking the gorilla, Leo Lion took off his head: It was Nick's colleague, wearing a lion's costume! He whispered: "Nick, Shhh …! Or they will fire us both!"
It looked like Mr Smith had had this idea before. But, where had the animals gone?

(169 words)

Notenschlüssel

Notenstufen	1	2	3	4	5	6
Punkte	80–68	67–55	54–41	40–27	26–13	12–0

Jetzt mal **BUTTER** bei die Fische.

Feedback

Liebe Kundin, lieber Kunde,

der STARK Verlag hat das Ziel, Sie effektiv beim Lernen zu unterstützen.
In welchem Maße uns dies gelingt, wissen Sie am besten. Deshalb bitten wir Sie,
uns Ihre Meinung zu den STARK-Produkten in dieser Umfrage mitzuteilen:

www.stark-verlag.de/feedback

Als Dankeschön verlosen wir einmal jährlich, zum 31. Juli, unter allen
Teilnehmern ein aktuelles Samsung-Tablet. Für nähere Informationen
und die Teilnahmebedingungen folgen Sie dem Internetlink.

Herzlichen Dank!

Haben Sie weitere Fragen an uns?
Sie erreichen uns telefonisch **08167 9573-0**
per E-Mail **info@stark-verlag.de**
oder im Internet unter **www.stark-verlag.de**

Erfolgreich durch die Abschlussprüfung mit den **STARK** Reihen

Abschlussprüfung

Anhand von Original-Aufgaben die Prüfungssituation trainieren. Schülergerechte Lösungen helfen bei der Leistungskontrolle.

Training

Prüfungsrelevantes Wissen schülergerecht präsentiert. Übungsaufgaben mit Lösungen sichern den Lernerfolg.

Klassenarbeiten

Praxisnahe Übungen für eine gezielte Vorbereitung auf Klassenarbeiten.

STARK in Klassenarbeiten

Schülergerechtes Training wichtiger Themenbereiche für mehr Lernerfolg und bessere Noten.

Kompakt-Wissen

Kompakte Darstellung des prüfungsrelevanten Wissens zum schnellen Nachschlagen und Wiederholen.

Den Abschluss in der Tasche – und dann?

In den **STARK** Ratgebern findest du alle Informationen für einen erfolgreichen Start in die berufliche Zukunft.